CURSED ECHO

INFERNAL PASSAGE

GAY LE

Copyright © 2021 GAY LE HAMMOND

Proisle Publishing

1177 Avenue of the Americas, 5th Floor, New York, NY 10036, USA

info@proislepublishing.com

ISBN: (sc) 978-1-7376654-1-0

PROISLE PUBLISHING

THERE IS NO SUCH PLACE AS HELL.

HELL IS "*JUST HEAVEN*" FOR BAD PEOPLE.

TABLE OF CONTENTS

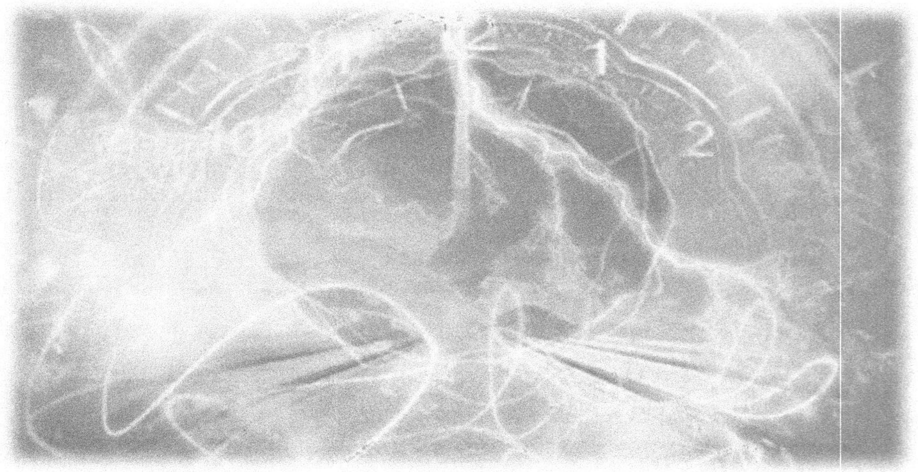

CHAPTER ONE

WHAT WE'RE REALLY MADE OF

Within your liver is billions of cells. Each cell is an exact replica of each other. Each cell is responsible for the ongoing re-generation of your liver every six weeks. This ongoing cycle of reincarnation continues over and over again, same time, same age, same impact, same reactions they are immortal. Without one of those cells, your liver would not function properly.

Within a droplet of blood is over 50 billion cells. Within each cell is a minute atom and within that atom is an individual consciousness or awareness. Each consciousness a fractal mathematical equation filled with the knowledge of everything within the entire universe; past, present and future. Within one of those cells is another 50 billion cells and atoms, within each one of them is another individual consciousness. Each contains the same fractal information of the whole. This continues endlessly, forever. There is no beginning; there is no end, making everything in existence immortal.

Every miniscule component of each atom is made up of mathematical binary codes. Every binary code syncopates intricately with the matrix binary of the entire universe. That is why you live in your house, in your street, in your neighbourhood, in your town, country, world, solar system, milky way, universe. Every algorithm throughout the universe syncopatesperfectly.

That is why you live with your family. Why you have your friends and enemies and will be educated a specific way, chase that specific career, marry that person, have those children, divorce that person and marry another, drive that car.

That is why you will become a rich man, poor man, beggar man, thief, the colours of your skin, the health of your body, your diet, your addictions, your love life. You may become a sailor, a murderer, a paedophile, a victim of suicide, a miscarriage, a cot death, victim of a war or genocide. Every single passage of life has a specific binary code depicting its direction and every single cell within your body has the full story of every dramatic incident that has taken place since the beginning of the beginning of time and before.

The laws of the universe stipulate Karma equates as cause and effect, opposite and equal value, likes repel and opposites attract. These rules dictate that everything throughout all existence will continuously act or react to its surroundings forever. This includes the human form and every individual cell within it.

As the universe acts and reacts the matrix binary upgrades and alters and so does the physical appearance of everything within it. The more the universe evolves the more detailed and complex each universal matrix becomes.

What has never been suggested to date is, we as universal creators are also responsible for those reactions which created the laws of the universe. Through our impenetrable emotion of fear, we have created the ongoing universal regulations. The consequences of that fear are now 'like repels and opposites attract' indicating our ongoing need to fight in all situations.

Recent evidence has shown that when the underlying creative emotion is not fear orientated but one of self-respect and self-empowerment, and self-love those laws alter as well; like binaries then attract and opposites repel. creating a universe of love. What this determined was that the entire outer universe we see, is also only a reflection of all our inner cells and who we truly are.

Most people know the basic story of **Roger Bannister**, who, on May 6th, 1954, busted through the four-minute mile barrier with a time of three minutes, fifty-nine and four-tenths of a second. The time factor then was determined in hours, minutes and seconds. Today we altered the space continuum from mileage to kilometres and the time space from minutes to macro seconds to nano seconds. This record is now broken regularly. It is simply a matter of perception. As Einstein says, "Until we needed it, we don't look for it. It is always there. We simply didn't need to create it yet."

The significance is that every human's binary code is translated to the most miniscule of nano encryptions. Every specimen throughout the universe is a binary coded emotional garment made up of unimaginable amounts of cells. We are cells for blood, we are cells for bone, we are cells for muscle, organs, skin and brains. It doesn't matter where you scrutinize the human body, you will find nothing but millions of miniscule cells.

Within your liver cell, before it is reincarnated, are billions of other nano cells that determine the path of this cell, so it is able to follow to reincarnate to upgrade your liver at the syncopated time, then follow throughin six weeks' time to start the degeneration process by dying. This is the ongoing rhythm of all life or history repeating itself.

Reincarnation and its many stems have been an interest of mine since the early sixties; life between life experiences, past life regressions, near death experiences, and anything to do with the afterlife or death. Combining hypnosis with reincarnation personally became a full-time passion in the nineties opening research to new theories on immortality, reincarnational continuums, ongoing lives, binary codes and universal codes that are defined by the universal laws. Then the discovery that a consciousness of infinite cell throughout the entire universe exists by the fractal maths of those laws within them.

Combining all this new information exposed the how, when, where and why all the comeuppance that keeps happening in the world keeps happening and how. We, through our thinking, speaking and reacting, are responsible for all of it. However, the matrix binary which is your higher consciousness if you like, is responsible for our thinking speaking and reacting.

It also explained how every individual is responsible for *their* world only and how your higher consciousness translates the binary codes though us, by speaking though us and thinking though us, divulging every binary equation both within us and surrounding us only. That amazing breakthrough for me, exposed one of the biggest debarkles in history.

We are both yin, yang, male female in one cell. What this research revealed is that, all the great spiritual leaders of yore who stated they were speaking to some god, then dictated principles that man was a supreme being and woman was an abomination, was in fact informing his higher female consciousness within him of his interpretation of himself, for himself and to himself, for their individual journey alone. It had nothing to do with the rest of the world, only him.

The fractal maths within every cell memorizes dimensions that you cannot begin to comprehend, that span back beyond your imagination to the endlessness of all universes and time and never stop. To make that easier to interpret. In quantum, there is always a plus 1 in every direction. Everything and everyone are endless, limitless, infinite and eternal. That means we as boundless amounts of cells are immortal and simply keep upgrading, regenerating and returning over and over again.

Our binary codes encrypt our emotional reactions, alter our DNA and chromosomes, then immediately, physically transform us into the emotional personification of that reaction. Then as humans, it proceeds to communicate through us and to us as that emotion, exposing the emotional garment we are wearing. Easy translation is the instant emotional adaptation from sadness to laughter.

At all times your binary codes and the universal matrix binary codes are informing you of who you are and your function. Every thought, word and reaction are for you, to you, and about you. Your binary instantly encodes your DNA. Then, through your chromosomes, you are transformed into the physical personification of that thought, word or reaction.

Your higher consciousness syncopates your binary codes and the universal matrix to translates your entire surroundings, people, places and happenings, to expose to you your every thought, word and reaction. They are your feedback.

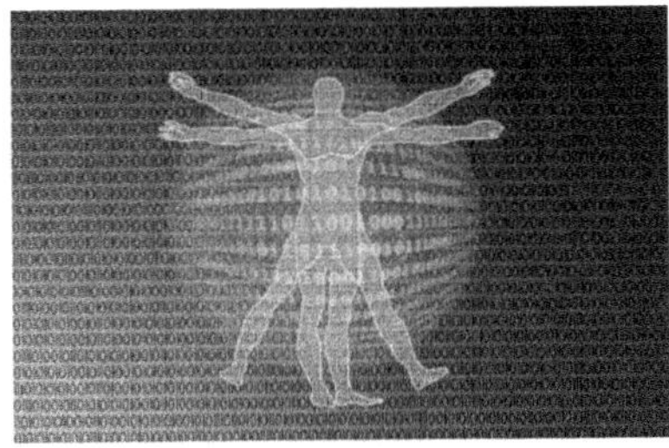

Your physical body is then surrounded by your auric field. Your auric field is compiled of all the binary codes of the matrix data dating back to the beginning of all time in every existence. From these histories your future paths have been determined based on cause and effect and all the Laws of the Universes.

This matrix binary field is your higher consciousness, it is what matches and deciphers all your feedback to you through your environment and surroundings at that time for you to interpret.

For example, if you feel angry inside and you do not understand why, your surrounding world *will* inform you. Your universal matrix or your higher consciousness match with your personal physical binaries at every moment to reveal your situation. You will uncover something in your surrounding world of the same format to give you feedback.

The old translation was, "You emit an emotion and that emotion will return to you in mirror formation the explanation". But in today's terminology it is much simpler and more theoretical. Your binary codes alter adjusting you and your outer binary matrix to comply. Your surroundings will explain your emotional state.

You may assume you are angry because someone was late. What your environment will explain to you through some arrogant person complaining is, you are angry because you cannot have what you want when you want it. You have been inconvenienced. You feel you have lost your personal power, your independence. What your environment will be informing you is, you are a victim of your own emotional lack of control. You are reacting out of anger to your own emotional garment. This format of disturbance will continue until you learn that you are doing this to you.

Next are your visual feedback fields or the visual form of the matrix field. These are the who, how, what and where you match. These include your close associates, family, spouses, friends, work mate's, social friends, enemies, workplaces, cafes, countries, and politics. These are your physical visual data and past life information revealing to you the paths you have taken and the future paths you are pursuing.

You, through your emotional reactions, good bad or ugly, alter your binary codes re-creating a new garment filled with those new reactions, and now you have to experience the entire scenario again incorporating these new reactions. Same actions, same reactions, same age, same time, same words only in opposite and equal value in your near future or next life.

In other words, we live in constant action replay over and over again like the liver cell. At a specific age in your past life, you carried out a specific reaction in male format, now in this life at the same age you will re-experience the entire reaction from the opposite perspective of female format. Depending on the intensity of your emotional reaction in each lifetime will determine the outcome of your next experience in each new existence thereafter.

Your human form or emotional garment of data is echoed from you and mirrored back to you by those around you. They do not actually exist in your universe. Their binary codes were replications of the same emotional reactions creating a similar path as you. If you react to them, you are followingthem; if they react to you, they are following you. They are both predicting your future path.

You and they, have reacted to your environment, in the same way to inform both of you of the specific emotional path you both are now following. You echo your emotional situation out to them, and they mirror it back to you.

They echo exactly the same emotional situation out to you, and you mirror them.

The difference is the interpretation of the original emotional discretion. When a teacher asks her students to write an essay about a day at the beach, every student will have a different story under the same title according to their interpretation of what they experienced.

To complicate this even further, when you look in the mirror, you do not see the same person they see. It is simply personal perception. The emotional disturbance you see in them is an emotional mirror of your victimised status at that time.

In an experiment last century, when the cell was split and they were placed in separate rooms kilometres apart, what they discovered was, whatever reactionary experiment they performed on one cell the other reacted in exactly the same way, at exactly the same time, with exactly the same impact. What they also discovered was the original cell had 50 million cells within it before being divided and both cells had 50 million cells in them after they were divided.

This action occurs with every cell throughout the universe. This information also explains the reactions within every cell within you. The ramifications were immediate; the adaptions were immediate and the emotional transformations were also immediate. What this experimentdetermined was the immortality of every cell in existence seen and unseen. Death does not exist. So, if death doesn't exist, what does?

Surrounding you next is your outer exterior experience. This is defined through your universal matrix or unseen cells (higher consciousness). First our towns, suburbs, areas and environment where you live. City, rural, mountains, valleys beaches, these are all your data and information imprinted by your binary necessary for your emotional experience. The ambiance of the environment around you stipulates the ambiance within you.

Edgar Cayce would explain how different areas of the world contained different energy vibrations. He would explain to his clients how they had to exit specific areas in order to recover from unacceptable lifestyles or illnesses. Through hypnotherapy, he was able to visualise the different emotional ambiances of the land. The vibrational energy of the earth is like everything else in existence. It has a force, a vibration, a binary code and it varies around the world and like all forces, the universal laws apply; likes repeland opposites attract.

Through your matrix data stored in your auric field you have been strategically placed or mathematically adapted to your habitats to explain to you the emotional status you are bound to.

Similar to the binary codes for the liver, they are in sync with the liver, not the heart nor the kidneys, therefore, it will create the necessary ongoing information to be placed where it needs to be placed to regenerate the liver only.

You, through your linked binaries, will generate the emotional reactions necessary for the universal matrix to place you exactly where you need to be to experience the path you emotionally generated from your first emotional reaction. This is the oneness of all things, worlds within worlds.

Also, as part of your universal matrix is the outer world, spanning out further is your country, north, south, east or west. Due to past life reactionsyour binary codes determine your philosophical allegiances. Your belief systems will from these positions determine your ethical and moral values. From this data you have a world value, an earthling value.

If an alien should invade, they will see a species of earthlings. From that perspective, they will evaluate each individual specimen; however, we will be put in boxes according to their belief systems which may or may not concur with ours.

As an earthly being you are the unseen component of our solar system which contains a multitude of planetsof varying degrees surrounded by moons and asteroid fields orbiting one sun. Our solar system is completely lost within our huge galaxy of the Milky Way which makes your earth also completely unseen in the universe. Our invisible planetis smaller than space dust. It is similar to a grain of sand 750 kilometers under the beach.

Our entire solar system which is gigantic to us is a mathematical deduction situated on the arm of Orion. This was estimated through Hubble from the view of the Milky Way from earth's perspective. However, from a universal perspective we are invisible. We do not exist. Yet I know we exist, and I know the billions of unseen cells within my body that I cannot see also exist. This explains the theory of the unseen cells and the impact their binaries too have on our matrix field.

In four billon years, the Milky Way will collide with Andromeda. Will the invisible speck of dust known as earth slip through or will the radiation of the collision completely shatter it into another billion pieces throughout the universe again? As a grain of sand, you imagine it slipping through; however, when we imagine our planet, we see its total demise and destruction due to our interpretation of the size of the planet. Simply perception.

All those galaxies within the universe are part of an even bigger cosmic consciousness which is another component of an even larger consciousness within our cells; it is never ending. **All** that information is stored in the binary of your little cell in your liver.

In every nano miniscule cell throughout the universe is the same fractal math equation that deduces a component of the whole. From that information, every cell has the necessary data to mega multiply into unimaginable endless possibilities. Your human path as an intricate cell is also predetermined, and your environment is informing you of the predictive path you have taken, and are yet to experience.

All the emotional stresses you feel are reactions from that original underlying emotional source of judgement centuries ago. It may be injustice, victimisation, or low self-worth. Our biggest fear is our dire need to survive. The survival of the fittest, the fear of dying. This is your under-garment of fearand through it you justify all your decisions from every perspective of that emotion.

This is the cornerstone of your personality or who you are. That powerful underlying emotion that determines all your reactions. The name of the emotion is irrelevant, it is the emotional feeling within you that dictates all your future paths. That emotion is connected to your innermost being, your inner most desires. It informs you in every existence that you will experience this existence and all your future lives through this personality.

For example, if you are a misogynistic personality every detail of your life will be dictated from the emotional feeling of extreme male dominance, whether you are male or female. The word is meaningless. It is your emotional feeling of that word that makes the decisions.

Depending on your emotional reactions at a time of any unacceptable encounter, your binaries will alter your DNA instantly and you will automatically respond barbarically to any unacceptable behaviour. You and the behaviour transform into one.

The personality of each person's garment is determined by our personal emotional judgements through each lifetime. When you react to anything, any person, any action, every cell within your body is transformed immediately into that reaction and you physically become the personification of that emotion.

You will then be completely digested by those emotional judgements and they will define all your decisions, your lifestyles, your family, your finances, your career. You altered your binary, your core information centre, now that new information will personify you.

Your judgement may occur because you have heard, seen or are a part of an unjust murder, according to you.

What you interpret as happening and what is happening are two different events. Through your personal judgement, you may stand up and protest. You may demand justice, validation, vindication, you may start fighting for the righteousness of the victim.

Rule number one is; the only reason this incidence is occurring in front of you is because your personal binary codes matched the binary codes of the *injustice* of the murder. The codes of the *injustice* of the murder and the codes of your inner binary are alike and you syncopated.

Rule number two is; you are repeating this occurrence again at the same time, same age and same impact as you did in your past life. If you react again your binary will alter, upgrade and evolve, thus transforming you even more into your ongoing personality of the murderer to continue in your next existence.

What this incident is informing you is your interpretation of the *injustice* of the murder is already within your binary codes. However, it is in the fighting against the injustice that you empower your own inner unjust emotion even more, exacerbating your binary codes even more, and transforming you more into the binary personification of the murderer.

In our one perception of one life where our judgement is an act of accusing and defending the innocent, no laws of the universe are entered into. However, the truth is, we actually have it back to front.

Your outer world is exposing the underlying emotion that is within you. You are actually fighting you. This is the mirror of your own inner injustice and the more you struggle the more empowered the perception of your fear becomes, allowing it to devour you completely. It may take several lifetimes, but eventually you will become the very personification of your accusation of the injustice of murder.

With each individual struggle you relinquish more of your own personal power. You become more victimised by your own personal beliefs. With each fight you become more like your assailants. You react and fight more in each lifetime. You slowly transform more and more into the personality of your assailant until you yourself become completely consumed by a binary of injustice liken to that of the murderer.

Unless there is divine intervention, the path of the murderer is your determined future path. You do not control the path, the path guides and controls you.

The binary code of that specific murder is syncopated with the universal matrix and once you venture onto that path, you will experience it unto the end.

Once completed, your journey may now take another path as your new perception of injustice has you fending for your life against a paedophile. And so, the path continues until you realise your garment or personality is your constant fight against injustice, not the arena you exist in. You see the world through the eyes of constant injustice in its many forums. As such, you will continue on the billions of various paths of continued injustice either as a perpetrator or victim.

YOU WILL EXPERIENCE ALL THAT IT ISN'T, TO UNDERSTAND ALL THAT IT IS.

The path will continue until you realise that neither justice nor injustice really exist. They are simply emotional garments you choose to wear.

Through many centuries you may travel many different forms of victimisation or entrapments and each time your upgraded body, associates and environment will inform you of the path you have taken. Why?

YOUR OUTSIDE WORLD IS MIRRORING YOUR INNER FEARS.

The twentieth century granted women the right to study and research. I studied reincarnation as a reality. Many great affluent researchers previously developed and uncovered various patterns ventured by every person in existence. The regressions unfolded the path not only taken by our death but our perceptions of life as well. Our conscious awareness during our life is the same conscious understanding we retain when we die. We do not transcend to any higher awareness or a heaven when we die. We remain within the consciousness we created during our existence.

Lives are a continuum, we are immortal, but new development, growth and realisations are always acquired through our emotional impacts while in physical embodiment. By reading our feedback in our surrounding environment we are analysing how and what we created, thus, we can automatically alter, upgrade and render many of our past improprieties or create more acceptable future formats. Regardless, every existence acquires a newer higher conscious awareness.

Examinations of past life regressions have unveiled that from this new higher consciousness, we then are re-programmed to react exactly the same way only from this new higher perspective and repeat it all again. Better, stronger, more varied, higher, lower and each time we do, we along with all the syncopated people, places and things surrounding us now read our *new* surrounding feedback and expand the consciousness of our upgraded perception of injustices even further. In other words, we as the new emotion of injustice, simply evolved.

For years, I was taught that if we altered me, I would automatically alter my future situation. We do; however, only to a new higher level of our original emotional garment. If your binary garment is injustice, then you now look at life through the original injustice but from a more productive outlook. You have only altered your perspective; you haven't altered your core emotion.

What we neglected to add to our equation was that the universal matrix is also controlling your outcomes. You created it that way; it is reflecting you. Your personality of injustices is so in sync with the universal matrix that the matrix is also echoing through you, talking through you, acting through you and your outside world is mirroring those responses to that injustice through your Law of Attraction right back to you.

After our discovery of how our emotional judgement of an incidence magnetically induces you to follow the binary of that path, it clarified why murders, wars, violence and prejudice of all description continually exist. What it didn't explain was what created the magnetic attraction in the first place. The answer is, it always is "you."

The single path of injustice is made up of endless maze of nano emotional paths to follow. Each of these paths have been recorded in all the binary codes of your cells and the universal binary codes dating back billions of centuries. One infraction on your part and any one of these paths in their entirety are opened to you to experience.

Only last century, we were introduced to the Law of Attraction and the magnetic force it emanates. However, we still see it as a force outside of us. Due to this new information regarding binary codes, we now understand we are the magnetic forces that cause the attraction.

Our binary codes translate within us visual images of our loved ones, friends, work associates, enemies. All your visual feedback of some past emotional infringement of injustice, meaning someone accosting you, reverberates the same information as your inner desire that is now defining you.

Meaning each person, place or thing is exposing a different form of that emotional infringement and this is informing you that one of your past life judgements, for instance validation, was of this nature and that is why you are in that position at that moment. This was the nail that victimised you at that time in your past life in order to have you defending it again at this time, place and with the same impact in your life.

Each strain of emotional judgement varies massively from one another. There are seven billion different strains of each emotional judgement of injustice in front of you on the earth at this moment and no two are alike.

Every person in the world is a replication of all your inner desires. However, in saying that, when you start stressing different strains of your inner emotions, a person, place or thing will appear in front of you informing you of the particular emotion you are emitting. They are reflecting that same emotion at the same calibre. You are mirroring you. You fingerprint each other with one particular emotional attachment of a specific injustice. That can be a person, a place, a magazine, a TV show, sports, entertainment or social media.

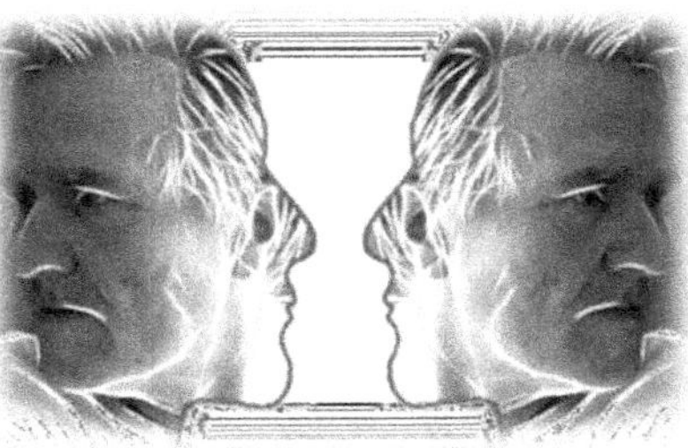

LIKE REPELS  **OPPOSITES ATTRACT:**

Every thought, word, action or event has an individual and specific binary code attached to it which determines its explicit path. It is your emotional reaction or response to your outer environment in each lifetime that dictates that future path.

As individual cells we are both genders, one seen, one unseen. Each existence we experience the alternate gender, this is yin/yang. Unfortunately, old philosophies have determined the human species as divided and existing in duality. This incorrect information is responsible for our inaccurate values today and explains why we exist as we do.

Because we see our world as outside of us as opposed to part of us, we have always judged our exterior existence as our nemesis, a menace, as opposed to our creation. Instead of attesting to our creative resilience and responding to it, we react to it as a danger, re-creating more of that imperiling situation for us to re-experience.

According to old philosophies, "ask and you will receive." By reacting to your surroundings, you are inadvertently and emotionally asking again. As a result, you will now re-experience the entire dramatic sequence of events you were reacting to, according to Karmic law.

LIFE IS AN ECHO.
WHAT YOU SEND OUT, COMES BACK
WHAT YOU SOW, YOU REAP
WHAT YOU GIVE, YOU RECEIVE
WHAT YOU SEE IN OTHERS, EXISTS IN YOU.

We keep looking outside of ourselves for answers, when the truth comes from inside. Understanding who we are and what we are will help us define where we are and where we are going.

Fighting for justice or injustice is the same thing. Your emotional discomfort is within your world, no one else's. Another of our deeming paths of injustice is revenge.

All paths of injustice are wide and varied pending on the ratio of other emotions attached. Gypsies had a cursed expression,

"REVENGE WILL DESTROY THE SOUL."

Every path of the reincarnational continuum moves forward. You have some people following and others leading. We are emotional garments defined as humans. Every word we speak is repeated from our past binary codes informing us of our specific direction. When a curse of revenge is instigated, the binary code is one of the threats of death, murder, assassination. If the accused is a murderer, a rapist, or abuser, because the accuser's garment becomes the same personality, the accuser becomes part of the final binary equation and will follow the path of the murderer to be murdered, or he could recognise his journey and choose the clean slate.

It is not the act of murder, war or impoverishment that we follow as much as it is the waves of emotional injustices attached to our judgement of specific situations.

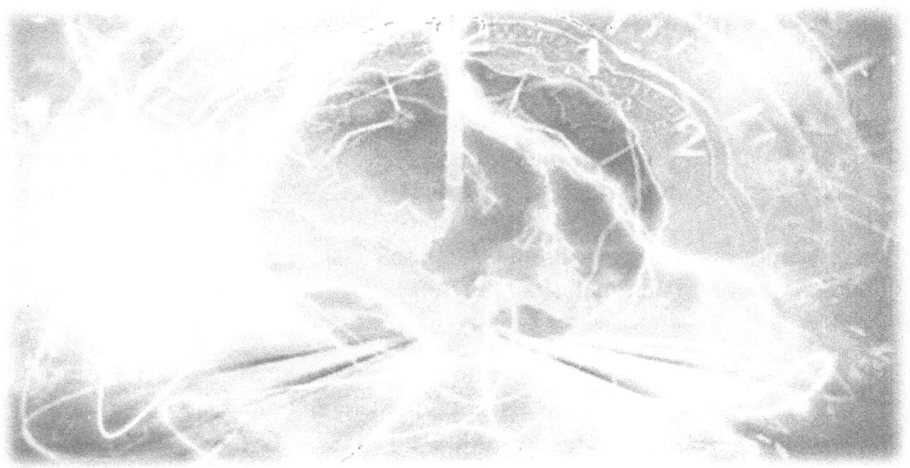

CHAPTER TWO

IT WAS NEVER ABOUT THE MONEY

Shackled in handcuffs with a two-policeman escort, Eli was lead from the court room for the last time. The nineteen-year-old child glanced back at the small gallery with a condescending smirk exhibiting no remorse for his actions. The overwhelming evidence made the verdict easy and conclusive for the jurors, 100% guilty. His sentence was yet to follow. Family members were stunned at the facts supplied by the law enforcers deeming it to be false and manifested because they couldn't find the real killers.

His older brother Liam sat in the witness's gallery bewildered and traumatised that such an atrocious act could take place in his family. His father was a hardworking provider. He owned and ran an international importing business from India. He was violent and cruel, but he didn't deserve to be murdered so savagely by anyone, let alone his son and his younger brother.

He watched his little brother struggle as he straddled out under guard to a van hidden out the back in a secured area ready to usher him away to await sentencing. According to the evidence this was no accident, this was a premeditated murder; he would be receiving the full extent of the law's punishment without parole.

As the doors slammed behind Eli, Liam saw the last of his family depart from him forever. The full impact of what had occurred was now weighing heavily on his shoulders and although the support from other family and friends was sincerely appreciated, he really wanted all the well-wishers to leave him alone. None of them could ever truly understand what he was experiencing.

The night of the unpleasant incident, Liam was out with a group of friends. It was graduation and he spontaneously decided to leave for the weekend's celebrations. Sitting in the court room, he pondered how his decision may have altered the situation or would he have become another casualty. Watching his heartless, unemotional brother throughout the trial, he listened to the substantiation of proof as they accused his brother of preplanning every detail leading up to and including the murder, followed by the huge cover up of evidence to blame another person who didn't exist.

Liam feared that had not a friend invited him away for the weekend he too could have been another statistic of this horrendous homicide, thus leaving his brother Eli as sole beneficiary of his parent's estate.

Liam's head was stupefied as if he was put under some evil spell. He'll wake up soon and this will all be a horrible nightmare. Less than twelve months ago his life was normal, now it's a huge paradox of bewildering chaos. It didn't matter which way he turned there was constant reminders of what was and now what isn't.

Happiness, fun, joy, all appear to elude him now. There's an ache in his being, he supposes it is his heart, but that would mean his heart is huge, for this incessant pain is in every inch of his physical body, and there appears to be no reprieve.

People are jostling him to move, to depart the courtroom. He knows he is in a daze. He has heard that expression about other people but now he is walking it. It is like walking in a fog. You can hear others around you, but the noise is a blur. You have no direction, no path, and although the world is still moving around you, you appear to have stopped still. What's more you don't have the emotions to care anymore.

Family members are surrounding and cocooning him away from the press as they want to know how he feels about his brother committing such a heinous crime. Is he happy with the verdict?

His uncle steps up and makes a statement pleading with the press to respect the family's privacy in this very difficult period. He then wraps his arm around his nephew as he huddles him off to an awaiting car. He too has now lost the only brother he has ever had. They appeared to be close and shared lots of family time together, but he as the oldest now has to be the strongest; theone the onus falls upon to support his young 23-year-old nephew in his time of dire need.

All the family were all going back to the uncle's house for tea, coffee and cake. Decisions had to be made. The sooner the better, the sooner this family would be able to get on with their lives. Liam didn't have the courage to return to his father's house anymore. The trauma of the night now depicted the house as opposed to the upbringing within the walls.

The night the police informed him that his father had been murdered in a robbery, he returned quickly to the house to see his parent being taken away in a vehicle bound for the morgue. He struggled through human barricades to enter his home in complete disbelief. He wasn't allowed to enter, only peek in to see the blood splatters up the wall and on the foyer floor. He declared his father must have caught the robbers unaware. They thought the house was empty and he came home early.

He remembered being huddled onto the front step surrounded by police, ambulance and people in protective gear all rushing back and forth passed him. His younger brother led him to an awaiting ambulance, covered him in a blanket and sat beside him with his arms around his shoulders,comforting him. Eli was so strong, and Liam was completely inconsolable. He would not have made it through the night if it wasn't for his young brother's compassion and strength.

Eli informed the police he came home from the club and found his father lying on the floor in a pool of blood. When he realised, he'd been murdered, he called them immediately. Eli was covered in blood but according to him, that was because he tried to revive his father. He inadvertently stepped in his blood when he found him and spread his footprints throughout the house. He had an answer for every one of their questions. Everything appeared to fit the robbery theory.

For months police followed through with their investigations and kept coming up empty. Then they started requestioning Eli again. They'dreceived a tip and called him in for more interrogation. He returned home again but within days criminal investigators were back and this time they had awarrant for his arrest. Liam protested and told Eli he would get the best lawyers; this was a huge mistake. However, he was to be proven wrong.

Evidence proved Eli had a visitor who saw his Astin parked around the corner late in the afternoon. He couldn't have been partying when he said he was. Although the witness didn't gain access to the house, she knocked several times and left. It was his car and it was the only one like it in the neighbourhood. She thought it strange at the time that it wasn't parked in the garage but around the corner in the lane for it was a very expensive car.

Eli took such pride in it. The concept that he would leave it out on a street was unfathomable.

The police came to the house and searched through his possessions. His phone, his computer, his car was all seized and used as evidence against him. All of a sudden this was not a robbery gone wrong; it was a first-degree murder case and young Eli was the prime suspect.

Liam's world had been shattered by the murder of his father but now it was completely falling apart. His entire family was the centre of an intense murder investigation. He had to get out, he couldn't stay in the house anymore. He agreed to move in with his uncle and when everything has settled, he will sell the house for whatever he can, and they will all move on.

The court revealed why the circumstances took place and they portrayed young Eli as a callous, cold hearted, greedy young man who committed a huge atrocity against another human being to satiate his avarice for money. If the justice system had their way Eli will never see the light ofday again.

Slowly and intermittently guests began to leave the uncle's house conveying their condolence to all the family as they departed, until finally the only ones left behind were Liam's aunt, uncle and cousin. His young cousin was a tech nerd and stayed out of everyone's way; he simply said good night and went to his room to get on his computer to play his games. This was how he dealt with everything, happiness, sadness, and family disasters. He was safe in this world of games and he knew how to control them. The real world was quite dissimilar and had a different set of rules, and his cousin really didn't know how to play.

Liam moved into his older cousin's room. He was working overseas and wouldn't be home for several months. He came home for the funeral but then due to business responsibilities had to return. This worked out well for Liam for it gave him the opportunity to move in until something better came along. Right now, joining his cousin overseas was looking like the perfect option, but he still had to clean up a huge mess left behind here.

Within another ten weeks the court would bring down Eli's sentence and the family would all have their opportunity to express their feelings both to Eli and to the court. The family would have the option to forgive or condemn, both are accepted within the court walls. Liam didn't want to say anything.

What he had to say to him would keep. He would tell him in private one day when he gets his courage up, not that he was afraid, but he was confused and angry at his brother's behaviour.

Truth be known he wanted to thump his brother; he didn't want to talk to him. Liam wanted to hurt him the same way he did when they would fight when they were young. Eli always had mum on his side. He would start fights to egg Liam on then claim innocence and Liam always copped a huge beating from his father because he was the eldest. The court was right, he was a spoilt little brat, and he probably killed their father because he couldn't get what he wanted again.

The court revealed that Liam's father told Eli as long as he was paying his university fees and paying for his car, he had to at least pass his courses. If he didn't, he wasn't going to pay his way anymore and he'd lose his car and all his privileges. He would have to travel and live like all the poor kids. He accused Eli of living off the lamb.

Eli felt he was too far behind and he'd never catch up. He'd have to do the last year again. His father informed him he wasn't going to pay for another year.

When the results of his courses came through, Eli passed poorly but he knew these results would not satisfy his father, so he hid his results to delay time and instigated a plan to install him as a hero in his father's eyes to alter his decision to pursue some study he wished to follow. He really wanted to sail. He always loved the water, even when he was a child.

Liam on the other hand was studying to be a research chemist; this has always been his dream. Eli's father, however, was forcing Eli to do business studies so he could carry on the family business. Eli hated the fraudulent business, and he hated his father for not understanding.

When Eli discovered his failing grades, he put in play a plan where he would create a burglary and save his father's life. He would then go to the club with his mates as an alibi then return later to find his injured father and cry for help.

He arrived home, checked out his brother's room but it was vacant, Liam left a note expressing where he could be contacted. This was the bonus Eli was hoping for and it gave him more time. He found his weapon of choice a large long kitchen knife left on the bench and he waited behind the entry door.

There was constant knocking at the front door from a university friend. He wanted her to go away before his father came home. He wanted her to think he wasn't home. It must have been the longest eight minutes inhistory. Finally, she departed. He breathed a sigh of relief.

Afternoon passed into early evening and Eli waited patiently pondering his plan of burglary in the darkness of the hall for another 40 minutes. He heard the remote-control door open and as perspiration covered his brow, he knew it would not be long now. Eli would injure his father enough to leave him unconscious then return later as the hero. The key was in the lock and the hall door opened. His father walked into the dark, dropped his keys on the side table and turned into the light where he saw Eli facing him. He wasn't supposed to see him. He wasn't supposed to turn around to see the knife, Eli panicked.

Eli thrust the blade into his father's gut once, twice, three times. His father's dark black eyes stared back at him as he clung to his son for life. He fell to the floor breathing his last. He died instantly. Eli froze, then adrenalin kicked in and he started thinking quickly. He had to stick to his original plan of the burglary, so he continued on with a plan B.

He had to steal his father's wallet and jewelry. He smashed several things around the house. He changed his clothes placed them in a garbage bag with the weapon and prepared to put it in the back of his car.

He had to get out of there quickly without anyone seeing or hearing him. He was now dressed to party with his friends at the club. He sneaked out into the dark lane to his car and without its lights on, he quietly drove down the back street. He drove into a nearby shopping centre with a huge garbage bin and threw all the evidence into it knowing it would be collected in the late hours of evening and continued on his way to join his friends at a club. He swilled some alcohol in his mouth pretending to be drunk from his pub crawl.

That night he was extra loud and boisterous so people would remember he was there. When the right moment arrived, he decided to leave and return home appearing to be incredibly drunk. Driving home he parked his car in the garage then re-entered the house. He screamed and yelled loudly so the neighbours would hear him. They would know when he came home. He called the police and within minutes they arrived. They needed to know the whereabouts of the older brother and everything that had occurred when Eli arrived home. All evidence looked like a robbery gone wrong.

Eli called Liam and when he arrived Eli was a tower of strength in Liam's hour of need. Their father's body was taken away and other family members were contacted. Their uncle came and consoled the boys encouraging them to stay with him at his place.

They remained up the rest of the night trying to absorb all the evidence and pain they had all just experienced.

For months, the testimonies were sending the police around in circles. Nothing added up. Then out of the blue a young woman came forward with new and vital evidence. She saw Eli's car in a strange place when he was supposed to be partying at a local club. This created a false alibi for Eli. The dexterous detectives started piecing his story together and there were too manyoddities that didn't add up. What if this wasn't an accident gone wrong but premeditated?

They bought Eli back in and requestioned him, then let him go again. They started re-examining the records for new possibilities and instead of theft, this produced a new case for the homicide squad. Finally, word came in from the local dump. They found the bag of clothes and what looked like the murder weapon. They had them forensically examined quickly and all the evidence pointed to Eli without a doubt. This was what they needed. They then proceeded to arrest him on first degree murder.

Liam accused the police of being too lazy and just accusing anyone now because they couldn't find the real killer. "I'll get you the best lawyers. They've made a huge mistake," screamed Liam as his young brother was taken away in police car with his hands shackled behind his back.

Weeks turned into months to nearly a year before they finally went to court. Liam moved back into the house and returned back to university. His mind still wasn't as focused as usual and he wasn't sure this was his path anymore. He was told to stay home but that would have been worse.

It was the waiting, the not knowing, that was driving him crazy. His lawyer said they had a good case, and this gave Liam confidence that his brother had been unjustifiably accused of a murder he didn't commit.

After five weeks of evidence in the courtroom from both sides of the court, finally the jury returned with straight forward answer. Guilty on all counts. First-degree murder.

As Eli stood before the judge he didn't flinch. It was as if he didn't believe he did anything wrong. He had no sense of what had occurred. He appeared to not care what others thought. Then they took him away and Liam was dumfounded at his brother's nonchalant performance.

Liam loved his brother. Eli wasn't capable of this type of assassination. But the evidence proved without a doubt that he not only was capable, but that he did.

Time passed and Eli received the full 25 years without probation. That would make him nearly 45-years old when he is finally released from prison, if he gets out. He would be place in an isolated prison with other hardened criminals out of human sight so the world would forget and get on with their lives.

But this was Liam's brother. He was not going to forget his brother. Eli was the only family he had. He would visit him regularly. He would not abandon him regardless of what other people thought. He just had to start.

With Eli in prison, Liam now inherited everything. The huge house, the importing business and all the money. He became one of the youngest wealthiest men in the state overnight. He went back to university and completed his Ph.D. He attained his doctorate in chemical research as well as head of the importing business. Liam was coping stupefyingly on his feet.

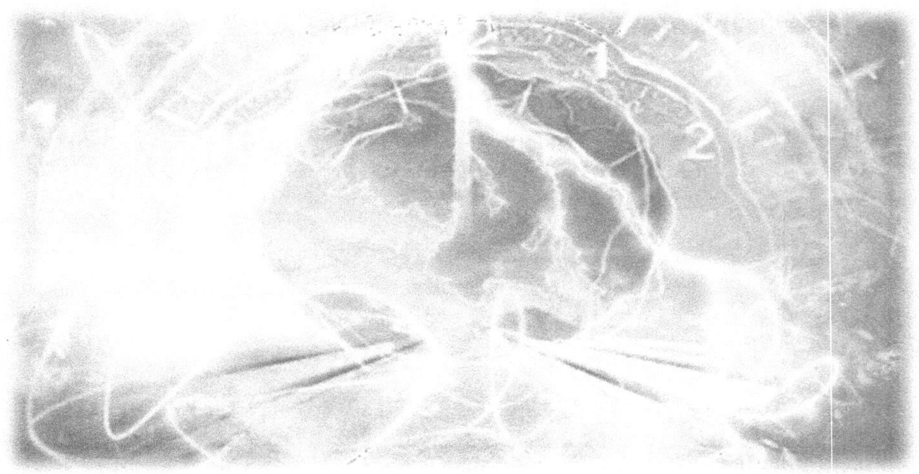

CHAPTER THREE

YOU LOSE: YOU'RE STUCK WITH ME!

It was the time of international trade by sea in the mid-sixteenth century. It was the evolution of ships against ships, country against country. Pirates were affluent in the Mediterranean region and many mariners were taken and never seen again. Father and son were at sea again. The dark-haired widowed Captain saw his enemy veering in on his colossal ship and but his steadfast vessel and crew were no match for shrewd Pirate. The Captain's young son was on board with him as a young cadet, and the Captain swore after the loss of his wife, he would protect him forever.

He would point his finger to his son and say with a large smile, "You lose. You're stuck with me" meaning he's got him for a dad whether he likes it or not and he swore to protect him forever.

Canons blazing, torturing swords flaying through the air both attacking and defending the pristine vessel. The Captain lost his unsullied ship to a far more highly skilled water rat. The crew were dragged on board the sleek attacking vessel and hidden down in the repressive prison barracks of the Pirate ship while the Captain's ship and its exclusive cargo were confiscatedby the buccaneers

The Captain's young cadet befriended a young cabin's crew member and discovered the hostages were to be taken to the nearby port to be sold. Upon arrival at the dock, however, both ships were set upon by the wharf soldiers under the ruling of a new government. The ships were both seized and all the Pirates and prisoners were jostled to the local hellhole on the other side of the island to be lost and forgotten forever for travelling the waters illegally.

It was called "the hellhole" for no one knew what went on down there and no one survived. The stench from the place was beyond any sewerage and most of the town's people abandoned the area years ago. It existed for the outcasts, lepers, filthy dogs and prisoners that would never see the light of day again. The civilized area of the island refused to acknowledge this part of the island's existence for it was too wretched.

The two abhorrent oppressors threw the scruffy Pirates and mariners of the King inside a pit and shackled them to the disintegrating wall and each other. Pirates and prisoners alike side by side. No toilets, no food, only the foul stench of human faeces and urine, mouldy bread, rats and vermin alike. The prison was manned by the Executioner, as he was called, who was a filthy pig of a human who could not speak properly and his disgusting offsider who was always amused at his masochistic friend's ignorance. They both enjoyed this world of sadistic violence and took pleasure in testing various appalling techniques of abuse upon their charges. The Executioner salivated at the creativeness of his abhorrent talent as he would procure piercing violence and agonizing torture upon his victims which fulfilled his hedonistic desires.

He would drool profusely at the mouth and his black hardened eyes cast the vision of hell with all its wretchedness and dereliction into his victims. His filthy hair was riddled with nits and vermin. He would scavenge the attire of his dead hostages as trophies upon his murdering rampages.

Food of mouldy bread and water would come every few days and the Executioner would distribute it upon his pleasure, knowing that the prisoners were starving and in pain. He would crowd them together so they couldn't breathe in the exhausting heat of the place. Dead bodies would be thrown outside onto the craggy street so the wild, filthy starving dogs could gorge on their carcasses.

The Executioner and sidekick displayed no empathy nor compassion, for as the prisoner's agreed, these barbarians had no heart or feelings of any kind. The Executioner was an animal who spoke no English or Spanish. He grunted to get what he wanted. He laughed like a hyena and was completely uncivilized in every fashion. Days dragged into months and many died from the heat or starvation. Occasionally, the Executioner would run his blade through one of his conquests because he was too weak to move.

The Captain and Pirate remained quiet as they twisted and maneuvered the long screws out of the incarcerating walls. However, the Executioner discovered another personal secret. One of the boys was the Captain's son. This ammunition gave the Executioner an insatiable passion to play and persecute in ways to traumatically distress both boy and Captain.

This was a new game for him and his offsider. The Executioner started taunting the young boy but as the boy began getting weaker his father found it more difficult not to protest.

Finally, the repugnant Executioner did his worst. His offsider dragged the lad over to the chopping block by his now long and filthy hair. With his final smirk of narcissistic sadism, the Executioner raised his filthy infected blade. With a huge scream of unrelenting pain, the lad stared into the callous unfeeling eyes of his slaughterer and saw the pit of hell within the demon as the Executioner horrendously laughed while he chopped off the lad'sarms midway between his elbows and wrists. The lad shrieked in shock and his father struggled for freedom and yelled all the blasphemy he could fathom at both of the filthy rotten uneducated swine. He would get free and when he does, both of those bastards are dead. This abuse only empowered the repugnant Executioner's humour of his dominance even further as he patronizingly danced around gushing in his victory.

Before passing out for the last time, the child swore a curse of vengeance on his persecutor for the Executioner too would die at his hands and it didn't matter how long it took. The cut-throat assassin laughed at his resourcefulness. He was thrilled as his offsider threw the partially slain body of the child into the corner like rubbish. The Executioner knew the kid couldn't escape; he was bleeding everywhere. This experience was exhilarating. He laughed as he scattered the breadcrumbs around for the prisoners to fight over with feet, legs, knees, any part of their body that would reach it.

The boy was one less mouth to feed. The lad was bleeding out profusely. Within days he started stinking as his arms became gangrene and covered with maggots. He was constantly in and out of consciousness until the Executioner had seen enough. Instead of killing his prey this time he would give his dogs live meat and fuel the antagonism of his father. Temporarily abandoning his safe haven to his offsider, the Executioner dragged the unconscious body of the nineteen-year-old child out into the street for his hungry dogs to devour later.

He brushed himself off, pleased with his ingenuity, he then casually walked away and left the carcass of the child basking in the hot, humidifying sun. He returned back inside to an unexpected reception. Standing before him in the middle of the floor was the Pirate with a huge smile on his face flaunting his captured offsider, as he indicted to the Executioner to look to his side.

Standing beside him was the Captain armed with the Executioner's toxic blade. Both Captain and the Pirate who were now substantially smaller in size were finally free from the shackles and now stood before him as his slayer.

The Captain located the Executioner's blade and when the sadist returned, the Captain swung the blade with all his might and anger. He swiftly and accurately cut off half of his head dropping him to the floor followed swiftly by the sidekick. Within moments the rest of the Pirates and prisoners alike began to make their escape together.

The Captain raced out to save his son. The jaws of six savage black mongrel dogs were vying for his body. One by one the Captain bladed their throats, but it was too late, his son was almost dead. "Save yourself," the child gasped with fainted breath.

"I won't abandon you," responded his father "you lose." The Captain picked up his son and carried his tiny starved little body cautiously through the scrub to nearby water. As no one anywhere else on the island was aware of the events that just took place, this escape appeared to be foolproof.

They uncovered their ships docked close by unattended, so they watched and waited until dark. The remaining crew all cautiously enlightened the faster of the two vessels with a new-found vitality and whatever strength they had. They waited for high tide and quietly slipped out of port. The island would be completely unaware of what had occurred for at least three days when the old lady came with the mouldy old bread.

The Captain bathed his son's body as best he could and wrapped his body in swaddling rags, but he knew he couldn't save him, so he stayed with him comforting and holding him till he died in the early hours of the morning. As he uncontrollably wept, he threatened, "If our paths ever meet again, you filthy swine, I will rip every piece off your skin off your body, I swear it."

The new crew of pirates and mariners alike wrapped the boy up in the rest of the swaddling then packed heavy cannons in the embalming with his body and dropped him into the deep water. As his son slid down a plank, the Captain pointed his finger and saluted as he said with tears in his eyes, "You lose," as the innocent body of his young son delved into the darkness of the water feet first never to be seen again.

The Captain stood on the deck as the ship moved away watching the space where his son was swallowed by the deep. His Pirate friend stood beside him, he beckoned to his young ship mate to bring something drinkable.

With a huge smile on his face, his First Mate bought out a bottle and said "Only the best." The Pirate laughed as he remembered the port where he acquired this magnificent brew, "Make sail." He was amazed how the brew happened to be still on the vessel and why it wasn't taken when the ship was absconded.

"Hid it; hid it good," gloated the First Mate.

He gestured to the Captain to have the first mouthful. The Captain swallowed and felt the smooth texture of the brew slide down his throat to his gut. His surprised expression spoke tomes.

"I know where there's more of that," remarked the old Pirate, and without saying a word they both knew their first port of call.

After several swigs the Pirate opened up, "Cap'n, I don't have a son and I know you're his sire but I'd be proud to call him my grandson, if that's okay with you? I kinda liked the kid; we all did. Ain't none of the crew that wouldn't have done anything to help the little guy, especially the ships First Mate. I think he'd have made a great pirate."

The Captain laughed. "Honour amongst thieves," he nodded and agreed as they both acknowledged the loss of his apprentice sailor and future Pirate.

The Captain decided to remain with his new pirate friends until they came to the roguish port of safety. "Barbarians alike here, but they are on our side." grinned the now rather scruffy skinny Pirate.

'A port, a Pirate, a pub, no money, no food and no potential,' thought the Captain as he scanned his surroundings and saw that his future prospects were looking extremely bleak to say the least.

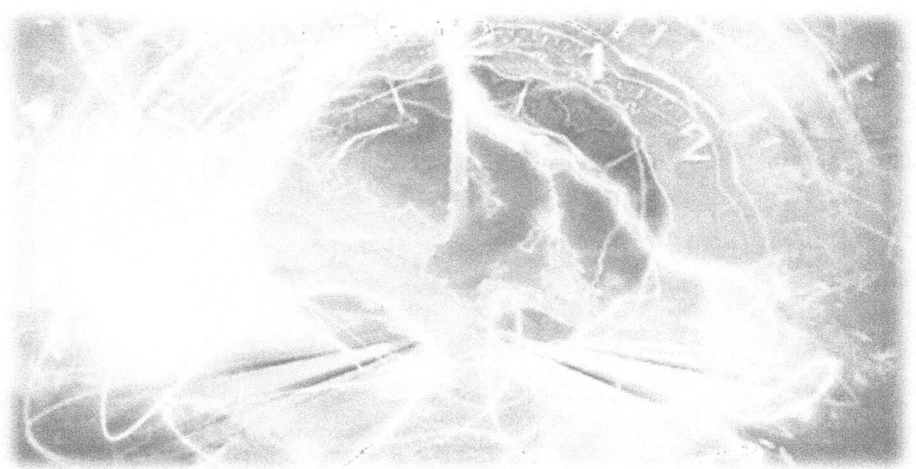

CHAPTER FOUR

THE PIRATE RECEPTION

They entered the heavily timbered bar dinned with noise, ruckus, fighting and brawling, all of them vying for more drink.

The reception went cold. The bar went silent as the escapees entered. Their audience thought themselves looking at ghosts. Their ships had vanished. No one had seen or heard from either of them for over three months. It was as if the ocean had opened up and swallowed all of them from existence.

"Three months?" echoed the Captain out loud. 'It had been three months; seemed so much longer.' Through the crowd barged the old mistress who owned the inn as she scurvily eyed them all up and down. The Pirate confronted her. "Get her away from us, she's a witch." Turning to the Captain, "She doomed me to hell."

The Captain quietly retorted as he scanned the room, "Well, you just escaped it." With sarcastic confidence he met the mistress eye to eye for he had nothing to lose, "No money, no cargo, but just escaped hell, so some great tales to tell for a bottle of brew and some broil."

The mistress scanned the Captain. She looked back at the Pirate. "You the devil?"

The Pirate pointed to the Captain inferring he was the one responsible for their remarkable escape.

"He calls me the witch," the mistress reacted with a cocky air, hoping to penetrate the same fear in him. Her hands were dominatingly perched on her broad childbearing hips.

Completely unfazed by her remark, he smirked, "You just inferred I was the devil," he sarcastically replied, greeting her eye to eye again, "we'd make a great couple."

"Ply them up," the old mistress cackled and yelled to the barman, as the last of the escapees beheld heaven at last. "You come with me." she beckoned to the Captain. He followed obediently. The apprehensive Pirate scuffled behind. He still didn't trust her.

She ushered them into a private room donned like fleet Captains' quarters. Captain looked around and impressively smiled as he felt quite at home in this cozy lodge. She ordered him and his friend a meal then offered him some scotch. As the liquor touched his lips, he tasted the same smooth warm distillation embrace the back of his throat. This was an impressive drop.

"You are the Captain?" she queried, as the Pirate stood up in protest. She blasted him, "No, you are no Captain. You led them into a trap, then he had to get you out. He is the Captain, or we have no deal."

The Pirate went to protest again when the Captain held him back. The Captain smiled at the mistress indicating he was interested, and he held up his glass demonstrating that another may seal the deal.

She rang a bell and after a few minutes in walked a mesmerizing young red-haired woman in Pirate's attire. Her eyes met the Captain's and she gasped for a breath. Her mother reeled and asked her "What do you see girl?"

"Feel." she responded. "He has sworn a path of vengeance on another who's soul is from hell." she responded uneasily.

"I told you." interjected the Pirate. "She's a witch. They both are." His Pirate friend kept protesting such a demonic business bond.

"Be careful you fool," the mistress forewarned, "for it is in the exact same words of your protest that you *will* walk that very path."

The Pirate shrugged his shoulders. "That'll never happen."

The young woman sidled over to the Captain who was now comfortably seated. "Your pain is from a broken heart. You wish to avenge his death, not his murder." Then she stood up suddenly and stepped back removing her hand as if she had been burnt, she announced. "You've already done it." she paused. "But now you are cojoined with another who has cursed the path of this murderer. You will travel with him until it is done. You must, you have bound yourself to him for all time until it is done."

"My son," responded the Captain as he angrily tried to catch his breath. "And I will."

She knelt beside him and explained, "To know such a love and devotion, one has to also experience its intense heartache." She placed her hand on his heart and smiled as she stared into his eyes she whispered. "Trust me."

The gypsy takes out a knife from her scabbard and with the other hand, takes the Captain's hand and sliced his palm, then does the same to hers, then binds both their hands together with her neck scarf. She takes the glass of scotch and pours it over both their hands

"Hey that's good scotch." he rebukes.

"Only the best," she smiles. "I will have your back too."

The mistress's daughter now reveals to them all their future paths together and the many lifetimes their paths will cross until it is done. Every lifetime will be a steppingstone to the next, to this final desecration which cannot be altered. The passion of revenge is the path that determines your journey, not your love. But it will be your love for your son that will save you."

She informs him of his bonds with the Pirates and First Mates and how all of them are on this same journey because they were present.

She offers scotch to him and them as a seal to always bind them. They take a toast, "ONLY THE BEST."

Mystique or not, the Captain wanted to see her again for she was a refreshing beauty. She explained they will meet again, but not in his life time. However, he will now always have her within him. They shared the rest of the scotch together from one glass, then the mariners departed.

The mistress glared at her daughter, "Do you know what you have done? You have bound yourself to this rabble man forever. Do you think he will love you the way he loves his son?" The old woman continued with her fury, "just because you lost your man to that malevolent whore does not mean you can latch on to the first man that comes along. She will walk her path of love and loss again and do it again, this is the whore's path. But be careful for she is linked herself to you she may even steal him, your Captain, what then?"

The gypsy responded. "He came to me. You didn't see his heart. It is the only way he knows how to love. To experience a love of that kind in one life time would be more than a gift. It would heal all hearts." Her mother could feel her darling girls broken heart. The gypsy daughter paused and then looked at her mother with a glint in her eye. "That man stealer has no understanding of a heart of this calibre. He would adore her and she would try to crush him. If

I have to, I will save him from her traitorous hands too. And you my darling ma' mom are bound to me in the same way. Interesting don't you think? That your love for me should be the same as his?" She smirked. "That's what bought him here tonight. He and you are bound in the same type of love; he to you, you to me. This night was verification of all our future paths together, including the whore." The gypsy mumbled "The whore had to take that fool from me so my real path could be revealed." Regaining her poise "We're only halfway. This perfidious path of hell started centuries ago and still has a long treacherous course ahead, and with each incarnation it will grow more intense until this terrifying path is finished and we're all travelling it together."

As the mistress sealed her scotch and replaced the bottle in her secret cabinet, "Not bloody likely," she rebuffed, "I'll probably end up with that disgusting little Pirate." She shuddered. "I know you are not supposed to judge, but that little warren rat is only good for my cat and she's dead."

A huge cargo deal was set and signed for by the Captain and his Pirate crew. This would now be his new life. He could not return home withouthis son as everyone assumed he was dead anyway.

His wife passed away several years before while he was as sea, that's why his son travelled the seas with him, so now there was nothing to return to. He raised a glass to the sky, "One day, maybe we'll get to say goodbye. You were a wonderful mother and loving wife; I fear I failed you both but I sincerely loved you both." Then he threw his wedding ring into the water. He was settled with his decision. "I have a new path and new family now. The Pirate, the crew, the mistress, the gypsy, they'll take care of me, cheers," he raised his glass to the heavens, then retired to his cabin.

The sleek Pirate ship raided many a cargo ship around the Mediterranean that was destined for the destructive port of ill repute. The Captain's intention was to make this port destitute. As many Pirates did, they succeeded in becoming the most renowned buccaneers of their time. It's not known if they were killed at sea or whether they simply vanished because they'd had enough, but the Captain and the Pirate always drank a toast to his boy every night with a smile. *"Only the best, forever"*

The gypsy was right about his son. The Captain threatened his path of revenge because his son's young death broke my heart. But being one with the gypsy, knowing she had his back on his dangerous path gave him the courage he needed to continue his treacherous journey.

"If I'm going into hell to meet this devil himself, she knows the directions. She knows the way out." He rubbed the deep cut on his hand and trusted it. He again stared out into the nothingness of the ocean; raised his glass, "Only the best forever." He pondered with a confident smile. "She'll save me; she'll save all of us."

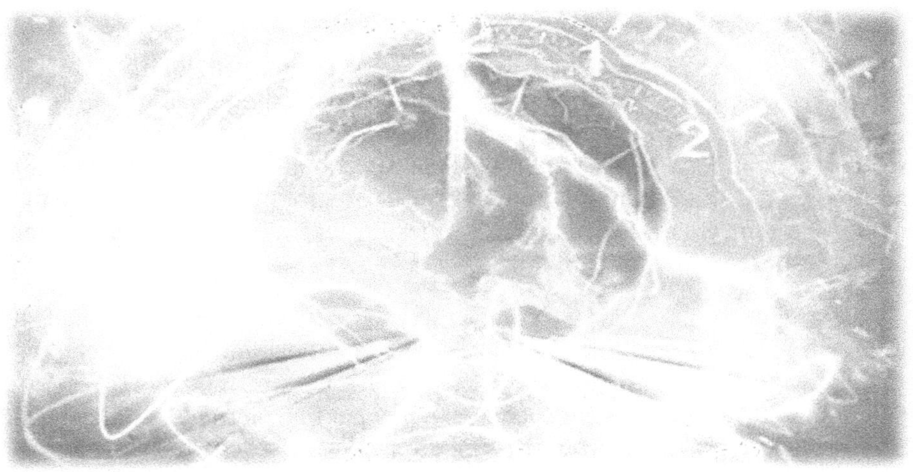

CHAPTER FIVE

NEWSREEL

Battle Scarred

WW1 had left its scars on middle Europe, and Germany wasn't going down without a fight. Warned never to create or build war machinery again, Paris, and most of Europe, stopped all forms of funding to be distributed to Germany. However, you never say no to a Narcissist, they will always undermine, steal and create in spite of your rulings, simply because they can.

Hitler's reign was to be the strongest Germany ever had after the first war and his nation was looking for a leader to save them from mass unemployment, huge inflation and starvation. What's more, the nation was desperate and didn't care how. It was easy to turn a blind eye when your saviour was putting food in your mouth, providing employment homes, and lifestyles within a regime for all families to be able to afford. He created an economy reversing inflation and productivity in a very short time.

This petty narcissistic leader was going to make Germany the supreme leader of the world. His aim was to give Germany back to the Germans and have the rest of the world succumb to his rule through whatever means necessary. He would build an army unsurpassed by any army alive. He would build a city of eloquence that the rest of the world would envy with art museums, roads airports, railways, and he would rule the world. No European establishment would ever be able to surpass him nor his new Aryan nation.

Balancing the Budget

Historical papers state in 1921, in the aftermath of the Treaty of Versailles, war reparation obligations upon Germany amounted to $33 billion. Keynes (1920) renown for Keynesian economics, strongly criticised the Treaty. It did not include any plan to resurrect the economy. Keynes predicted the punitive attitude and economic sanctions of the major powers against Germany would lead to new conflicts and instabilities, instead of seeking to secure long-lasting peace.

These reparations were in fact the origin of the calamitous events that followed; Weimar hyperinflation (1921-1923) and the dramatic impoverishment of the Bruning government (1930-1932). The resentment from the German population due to these disasters created a new unified German populace which supported Hitler's National Socialism.

When Hitler rose to power in January 1933, the economic situation in Germany was desperate. Stocks of raw materials had been depleted, factories and warehouses lay empty, and about 6.5 million people were unemployed and on the verge of malnutrition and starvation, while the country was crushed by debt and its foreign exchange reserves approached zero.

From 1933-1938, the resurrection of Germany's economy recovered spectacularly thanks to Schacht. His objective was to jumpstart the waning economy's which required money, but money was not available. Savings and production were non-existent. As money couldn't be printed, lending to the government would have put the Reichsbank at risk of losing control of monetary policy.

Schacht contrived a brilliant unconventional monetary solution. For payments, state contractors and suppliers received bills of exchange issued by a company called 'MEFO.' The MEFO-bills were state guaranteed. They could circulate in the economy and could be discounted by their holders at the Reichsbank in exchange for cash.

Schacht contrived that the duty of the central bank was to make available to the economy as much money as necessary to facilitate output production. The issuance of bills of exchange was instrumental to this end – as each bill stood against the sale of newly produced goods, and each issue of money was based on the exchange of the new goods, central bank money issuance against bills could not be inflationary. The employees of MEFO checked that every MEFO-bill issued was tied to a quantity of newly produced goods, and only bills issued against the sales of these goods were granted. This way, the circulation of money and the circulation of goods remained in equilibrium.

The Reichsbank undertook to accept on demand all MEFO bills, irrespective of their size, number and due date, and to exchange them for money. The bills were discounted at a 4% interest rate. As such, they were given the character of interest-bearing money, and banks, savings banks, and firms could hold and use them exactly as if they were money. If all MEFO- bills had been presented for discount at once, inflation would have resulted.But this did not happen, making the bills both re-discountable and interest- bearing allowed for much of them to be absorbed by the market without going through the Reichsbank.

Also, output responded remarkably well. State purchases fed into a growing demand for labour, and firms restarted investments using MEFO-bills as collateral for borrowing. Investments put additional manpower to work, and incomes and savings increased as a result, raising fiscal revenues.

In 1938, Schacht strongly urged terminating the MEFO program, as full employment had been reached and the closing output gap was raising price tensions. He clashed with Hitler on this, and on 19 January 1939, the Führer sacked him from the Reichsbank.

Such was the economic policy that allowed Germany to regain monetary sovereignty to finance its reconstruction in the interwar period, an *ante litteram* case of unconventional money-financed fiscal expansion. It enabled a national economy to exit a long and deep depression, and to attain non-inflationary full employment in a short span, all with no use of price controls or rationing in only five years. Schacht's program transformed the bankrupt state of Germany into Europe's strongest economy within five years, creating a country of untouchable supremism.

German Conspiracy to Ignite WW2

Much of what is known about the Gleiwitz incident comes from the affidavit of *SS-Sturmbannführer* Alfred Naujocks at the Nuremberg Trials. In his testimony, he stated that he organised the incident under orders from Reinhard Heydrich and Heinrich Müller, chiefs of the Gestapo.

On the night of 31 August 1939, a small group of German operatives dressed in Polish uniforms led by Naujocks seized the Gleiwitz station and broadcasted a short anti-German message in Polish. The operation was named *"Grossmutter Gestorben"* (Grandmother died). The operation was to make the attack and the broadcast appear like the work of Polish anti-German saboteurs.

To necessitate the attack to appear more authentic, the Gestapo murdered Franciszek Honiok, a 43-year-old unmarried German-Silesian Catholic farmer, known for sympathizing with Poland. He had been arrested the previous day by the Gestapo and dressed to look like a saboteur, then killed by lethal injection and given gunshot wounds. Honiok was left dead at the scene so that he appeared to have been killed while attacking the station. His corpse was then presented to the police and press as proof of the attack.

Several prisoners from the Dachau concentration camp were drugged, and shot dead on the site and their faces disfigured to make identification impossible.

The Germans referred to them by the code phrase "*Konserve*" (canned goods). In an oral testimony at the trials, Erwin von Lahousen stated that his division of the *Abwehr* was one of two that were given the task of providing Polish Army uniforms, equipment and identification cards. He was later told by Wilhelm Canaris that people from concentration camps had been disguised in these uniforms and ordered to attack the radio stations.

The Purpose of The Low Life's

The Luftwaffe performed a series of 360 to 400 experiments atDachau and Auschwitz, in which hypothermia was induced in 280 to 300 victims. These were conducted for the Nazi high command to simulate the conditions the armies suffered on the Eastern Front, as the German forces wereill-prepared for the cold weather they encountered.

Many experiments were conducted on captured Russian troops; the Nazis wondered whether their genetics gave them superior resistance to cold. Approximately 100 people are reported to have died as a result of these experiments. In early 1942, prisoners at Dachau concentration camp were used by Sigmund Rascher in experiments to aid German pilots who had to eject at high altitudes.

A low pressure chamber containing these prisoners was used to simulate conditions at altitudes of up to 20,000 m (66,000 ft). Of the 200 subjects, 80 died outright, and the others were executed.

Other experiments included: experiments on twins (such as sewing twins together in attempts to create conjoined twins), an experiment in repeated head injury which drove a boy insane. Experiments at Buchenwald where poisons were secretly administered in food. Experiments to test the effect of various pharmaceutical preparations on phosphorus burns induced with material from incendiary bombs. Experiments at Ravensbrück to investigate the effectiveness of sulfonamide after infection with bacteria such as *clostridium perfringens*, (the causative agent in gas gangrene) and *clostridium tetani* (the causative agent in tetanus). Experiments conducted to attempt treatments of chemical burns induced by mustard gas and similar compounds. Experiments at Dachau to study various methods of making sea water drinkable.

Many of the subjects died as a result of the experiments, while others were executed after the tests were completed to study the effect post-mortem. Those who survived were left mutilated, suffering permanent disability, weakened bodies, and mental disorders.

The results of the Dachau freezing experiments have been used in some modern research into the treatment of hypothermia, with at least 45 publications having referenced the experiments since the Second World War.

This, together with the recent use of data from Nazi research into the effects of phosgene gas, has proven controversial and presents an ethical dilemma for modern physicians who do not agree with the methods used to obtain this data.

Some object on an ethical basis, and others have rejected Nazi research purely on scientific grounds, pointing out methodological inconsistencies. In an often-cited review of the Dachau hypothermia experiments, Berger states that the study has "all the ingredients of a scientific fraud" and that the data "cannot advance science or save human lives."

Several Nazi experimenters after the war were employed by theUnited States government in Operation Paperclip and later similar efforts

.

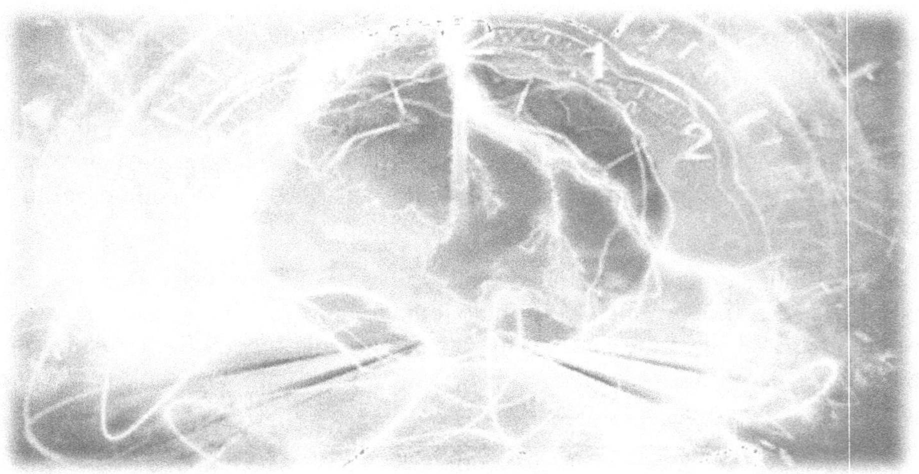

CHAPTER SIX

WHAT YOU SAY IS WHAT YOU GET.

After the initial invasion of Poland from Sept 1st 1939, many of the European prisoners over the next four years were taken and scattered to various areas of Germany for different experimental and trade purposes.

Being born on the wrong side of the Germans nationals had its penalties. After three and a half years of hard slave labour, a dark-haired prisoner along with many others were taken to a Dachau Camp where the researchers were working extremely hard on the effects of mustard gas. The strong looking prisoners were to represent the German soldiers in an experiment. They were stripped of their clothing and marched to an underground cement chamber with no windows and one door. They assumed they were going to be executed. Attached to the ceiling were pipes like gas pipes. The prisoners knew of the mass extermination of the Jewish people and were expecting the same penalization for them to take place.

They waited in the cold dark damp conditions, some young crying, some aged praying, the rest in silence. The room was soundproof so the other prisoners on the outside never heard the screaming. Once anyone entered this hellhole they never returned. There was murmuring of engines as motorsstarted churning, then showers of an oily liquid started spraying from thepipes. This was not water nor gas. This was like an acid and it burnt through the skin. It tore into the skin and it smelt like stale garlic and the prisoners gasped for air. As quickly as it started, it finished again.

Many collapsed to the floor screaming in agony, but the floor was saturated with the chemical so standing was the better option. The dark-haired prisoner stood strong and tall for as long as he could. He wasn't overly intelligent, but he was smart. He worked on his farm and kept his family in food. He had a strong loathing for the German race. They always thought themselves supremist to all other beings as they usurped all that didn't belong to them.

The excruciating pain of the burns intensified as many of the older prisoners started exposing second- and third-degree burns. Blisters, bleeding holes and sores began appearing rapidly. It seemed like hours before the door was opened. Those that survived were ushered to a prison dormitory where they were placed in hard bunk beds, four high. It was clean and sterile, however, no room to move. All researchers who entered were unidentifiable with covered masks and gowns.

The prisoners of war were forced to lie down flat on the bunks and be silent. Lying down made the pain worse. The dry hard mattress exacerbated the pain of the burns. When the prisoners would disembark from the beds much of their skin tissue was left behind or torn from their now incredibly deformed bodies. These experiments continued until a patient died or were deliberately murdered for further post-mortem research.

The beautiful strong dark-haired man was now a mere shadow of his former self. He'd lost all his curly locks and his wretched physique was flaying skin and bone. His torturer with eyes empty as black as hell enjoyed being abusive and tormenting. He enjoyed this sadistic research and saw these low-life vermin now as constructive. These animals were the scum of the earth and they had no better purpose than to serve the Reich for the highest good of the world. He held no sympathy or compassion for any of these biles of life. He shouldn't have to touch the filthy rotten scum; they were worthless to the world.

When young men who were in excruciating pain cried, they were belted by the guard to be silenced or given death in a needle for further post-mortem research. They were the first to be tested. All forms of chemical cochins were applied to analyze different research results. Nothing helped. Many died from their pain and burns, but mostly from shock. They were takenaway and they were never seen again.

The dark-haired man's skin started literally pealing of his skeleton. His fingers were skeletons with whipping clumps of skin hanging off them.The excruciating pain had numbed all his senses. He was starving but the more prisoners died, the more bread and water he received. He found it hard to swallow as his throat was no longer functional due to the burns. His esophagus was constantly in pain and many times he would regurgitate the little amount of food he mushed up in the water to swallow. He prayed it would finish. He wanted to die but not in their hands. He had survived the worst; they couldn't harm him anymore.

May 1943 there was hustle and bustle as things started rapidly changing. The smell of the inferno reeked the chamber as huge amounts of evidence and paperwork was being burnt. Researchers were being evacuated. Only the non-important scientists were sacrificed. Shots were fired everywhere as German guards tried to kill all the residue victims to hide the proof, but the shots didn't reach the dark-haired prisoners area. Then nothing. A deadly quiet.

Outside there were tanks barging through the front gates. Cheers of final victory were screaming outside in the fields. Noise was cluttering all around them, but the soundproof rooms remained silent. Then, finally a door was blasted open.

American and British soldiers began barging in screaming "Oh God! What's that smell? Medic, here! We need medics here urgently." As the medics arrived what they came upon disgusted them to regurgitating point. Human experiments. Officers tried to recover as many bodies as they could, while others went through the burning ashes to redeem anything that would inform them of what was going on here. They found a few live victims struggling to be saved. With what was left of his voice, the dark-haired man mimed. "Gas."

A mass grave was discovered out the back with thousands of skeletons thrown in on top of each another like a pile of dog bones. No names or identities were ever found. The dark-haired prisoner determination not to die this way had been achieved. He fought back with every ounce of fortitude that was within him.

The rescuers found files that verified some of their possible theories of mustard gas and other research. They discovered the researchers were using humans as live experiment to determine the effect of mustard gas. What they saw broke their hearts. Men and boys' bodies literally torn to shreds from the acidic elements of the gas. Plus, the reactions to the means by which they performed the test determined the magnitude the threating gas could destroy their enemy and how they could save their own treasured soldiers.

The extent of testing was only limited to their imagination. It didn't matter if they lost a patient there were always more working in the fields outside.

They were using other forms of chemical treatment for them. Poisoning their food to watch their effects so when the SS interrogated prisoners they would be more efficient. All was done to maintain and protect their pure race. These scums weren't pure and were allowed to be eliminated.

The German Aryan race was going to be the pure race and true race of the new world. Everyone and everything else were lessor and able to be eradicated.

The desiccated prisoner of war was bandaged and carefully carried out on a made-up stretcher and he was laid in the warmth of the sun, a vision he had not seen for many months. Through his blurry eye-sight he gazed up at his saving redeemer and saw he was not German.

The soldier returned his gaze to the shriveled victim of war and saw a hero struggling to survive. They both knew his time was limited.

The prisoner managed a smile through his wasted mouth which no longer had teeth nor lips. There was a glimmer in his eyes. He had beaten those demonic bastards. He mumbled with a smile. "You lose, you filthy swine." He felt he was finally free. The soldier looked around for his First Mate. When he saw him, he yelled "You got some of the sweet stuff? We got a little celebration over here."

His First Mate flashed his flask. The redeeming soldier bent down beside the casualty and whispered, "I know you don't understand me and you probably won't taste this, but I know you can imagine it. This is real smooth stuff. The best you've ever tasted. I'll put some on your gums cos my friend, after what you've been through sir," he then stood up saluted the martyr "you deserve only the best."

The soldier stayed with and comforted the gentleman knowing he wouldn't last long and placed several drops of the golden liquid on the gentleman's gums from time to time. They became acquainted and within a short period of time the hairless, skeletal fraction of a human, died heroically. He was buried in a proper gravesite and his first name was placed above his head on a cross. "Kapin."

A memorial plaque to many of the lost prisoners was placed on the prison entrance gate to remind the visitors of the horrific incidents that took place there under a reign of tyrannical third reich and their leaders.

Some of researchers were found and they confessed all on their day in court. Many were imprisoned and several were shot. Others were taken to American research labs where they continued their research with secret agencies to benefit the USA's undercover work for the cold war against Russia.

Many of the brave American and British soldiers left the European shores only to be quashed at sea by rogue U boats. The rescuing soldier and his First Mate were to become victims of such an ambush.

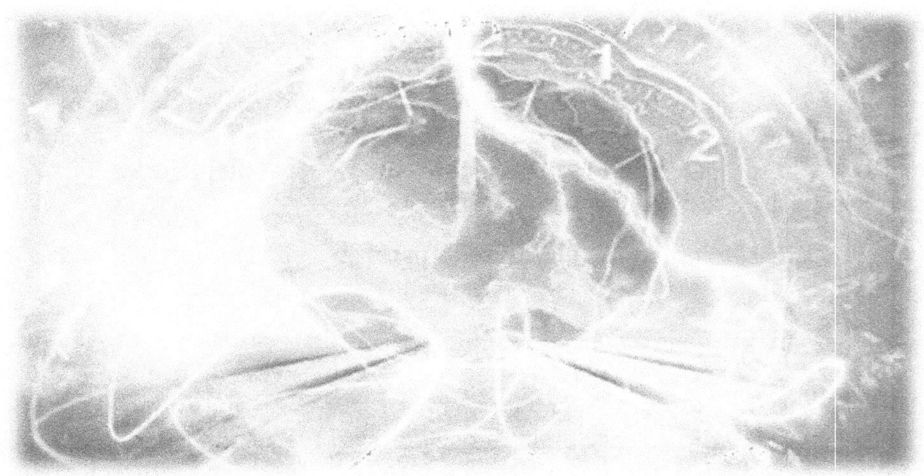

CHAPTER SEVEN

NEWSREEL

The Adopted Race

It sounds like the stuff of dystopian fantasy: Utopia means the fantasy of the ultimate happiness. Dystopia is exactly the opposite. Women volunteered to bear children to hand over to a totalitarian regime. But for thousands of Europeans, such a program isn't imaginary. It's the story of their lives. Approximately 20,000 victims are the Lebensborn, survivors of a Nazi breeding program designed to create racially "pure" children for the Third Reich.

Between 1935 to 1945, the secret program encouraged racially "fit" women to bear children for the Reich. These babies were thought to exemplify Nazi Germany's Aryan ideals and were protected. Translated as "fount of life," the Lebensborn program involved secret birthing facilities, hidden identities, and the theft of hundreds of thousands of children.

The program had its roots in World War I, which decimated Germany's male population and contributed to a sharp decline in the country's birth rates, which fell 43 percent between 1920 and 1932. This was a problem for Adolf Hitler and his Nazi Party, which came into power in 1933 with plans to usher in a new world order, one in which Nordic and Germanic "Aryans", whom were considered the most superior race, would rightfully reign supreme. In order to carry out Hitler's vision of a completely Aryan Europe, the Nazis would need to address the country's genetic shortage.

SS head Heinrich Himmler was convinced that abortion was the primary reason for the falling birth rates, and in 1935 he decided to strike back.

He decided to make abortions of racially "pure" children less appealing by offering an alternative to their mothers. Women who could prove that their unborn child would fit Nazi racial purity standards could give birth to the child in secret, comfortable facilities.

But there was a catch: Once the babies were born, they had to be relinquished to the SS. The SS would then educate them, indoctrinate them in Nazi ideology, and give them to elite families to be raised.

At first, Himmler urged the SS and German military to have children with Aryan women both in and out of wedlock, but as the war progressed, that became a mandate. When casualties further decimated the German male population, Himmler ordered his officers to marry and reproduce. Women in occupied countries were also encouraged to have children with German soldiers.

As the Third Reich moved eastward, it expanded the Lebensborn program to include wholesale kidnapping. Children thought to be racially pure were taken from their parents and temporarily placed in Lebensborn homes before being adopted by German families. In Poland alone, between 100,000 and 200,000 children were kidnapped; those who failed racial purity tests in Germany were sent to orphanages or summarily executed.

At its height, the Lebensborn program included dozens of birth centres in Germany and the countries it occupied. Comfortably furnished with the possessions of the deported Jewish people, these homes were quietly advertised as places where unwed mothers could escape social ostracism,ensuring a bright future for their children. In occupied territory, they were also a place to escape the fury of locals who faced starvation and oppression at the hands of the Germans, and resented the special privileges granted to women pregnant with "desirable" children.

It's still unclear exactly how many children were born in Lebensborn homes; current estimates range up to 20,000. However, that number may never be fully known due to secrecy on the part of mothers, incomplete and destroyed records, and new names given to children who were placed in Nazi families.

What is clear is the trauma suffered by children who were part of the program. After the war, Lebensborn became social outcasts both inside and outside of Germany. At the time, single, unmarried mothers were seen as social misfits, and in occupied countries, those who had engaged in sexual relationships with German soldiers were seen as traitors.

Education and employment opportunities were rare for Lebensborn. The government sent many children to different countries in an attempt to get rid of them, and many ended up in children's homes after their mothers were shipped off to concentration camps. Norwegian Lebensborn also allege they were used in secret military trials of drugs like mescaline and LSD; however, those claims have never been officially recognized.

In 2002, Norway offered about \$31,000 to Lebensborn to make amends for the government's treatment of children, but the country has never officially apologized. No other country has offered to compensate victims, who endured shaming and trauma. Those who knew they were Lebensborn faced the harsh reckoning with the knowledge that their fathers, and possibly their mothers, were devoted Nazis. But perhaps the most horrifying part of the program is the fact that so many people who were kidnapped or adopted under Lebensborn ideology will never know their true identities. The Nazis never managed to create an Aryan super race, but their quest for racial perfection, ironically, damaged a generation of the children they claimed to cherish.

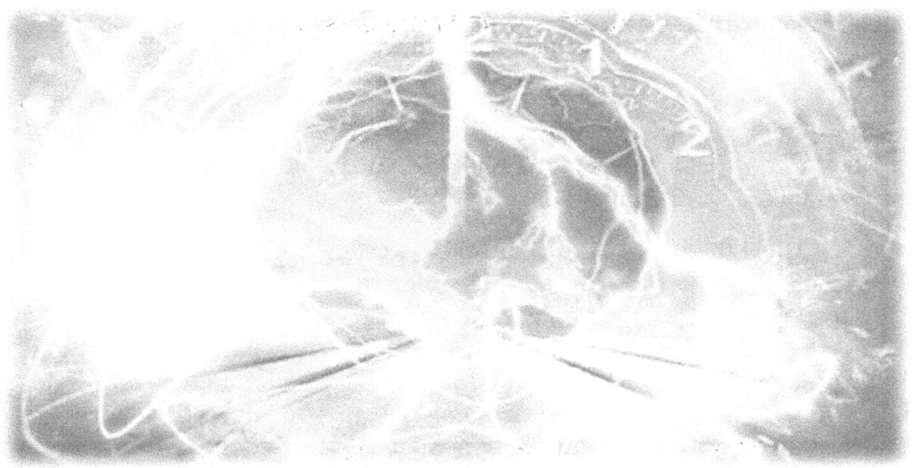

CHAPTER EIGHT

WEAVING FUTURE HATRED

Blonde hair, blue eyes, lean body lines, perfect specimen, he was eight. His family were imprisoned to work as slaves in the fields and he was legally kidnapped to build the perfect Aryan race of soldiers who would become the leaders of the New European nation under German Aryan rule.

The SS took him and later he was adopted by a German family. He was placed in a camp academy where he would be educated and taken care of as one of the "desirable" children. He was schooled every day about the importance of being part of this superior Aryan race. The furher was their supreme leader.

The student had his uniform; he had his books that taught of the Aryan dictatorship of supremacy. Their diet was to the benefit of their body. They studied daily, they exercised daily. There were no birthdays. They were all reborn on the day they arrived at the training camp. They all celebrated together. They thought as one. Their strength was in their unison, beauty, strength and superiority. They would only breed with their own kind and this would be arranged at the appropriate time to maintain the perfect order.

Every day they were drilled and brainwashed with the racist belief of their supremacy over all other breeds. They adopted the theory that European subservients, Negroes or dark native were monkey men. They climbed up in trees and flew from branch to branch. The Germans soldiers literally called them "Monkey men," to undermined the intelligence of the more superior enemy by informing them "this was the reason they were caught and why they would lose in that war. It was because of their lower intelligence."

This depiction of the German's interpretation of mankind was reported at the triumph of WWII when the same band of Americans who had been captured by the Germans near the front at the end of the war defeated the German narrow-minded ignoramuses.

Once the war was over, all the adopted children were ostracised and experienced endless forms of the human humiliations from everyone. So, all three nations scattered the young terrorists across the world to outcast prison camps where they would be forgotten; and they were. They found it difficult to find work, and to be accepted by nations everywhere around the world due to their strongly indoctrinated brainwashing. Many of them carried their bigoted biased and racist theories with them and inadvertently spread it across many countries for many decades.

Others who escaped the prisons died from isolation, poverty and detachment in a strange country after being so closely associated with their own kind for such a long time. This was to be the destiny of the young fateful student. His binary has altered, upgraded and advanced. He now wears a garment of supercilious hatred, abhorrence and utter lack of respect for all other breeds of human. He knows how to look his enemy in the eyes and kill him without any remorse or feelings of regret.

However, due to the demolition of his nation, he no longer belonged anywhere, he became a street rat and suffered from extensive starvation and desolation. He no longer had the unison or security of his pack. In his caged secure environment, he was free, in the outside world he was cast as a murderer. The loneliness and impoverishment crushed him to desolation and he finally killed himself by slitting his throat with a blade at the age of nineteen.

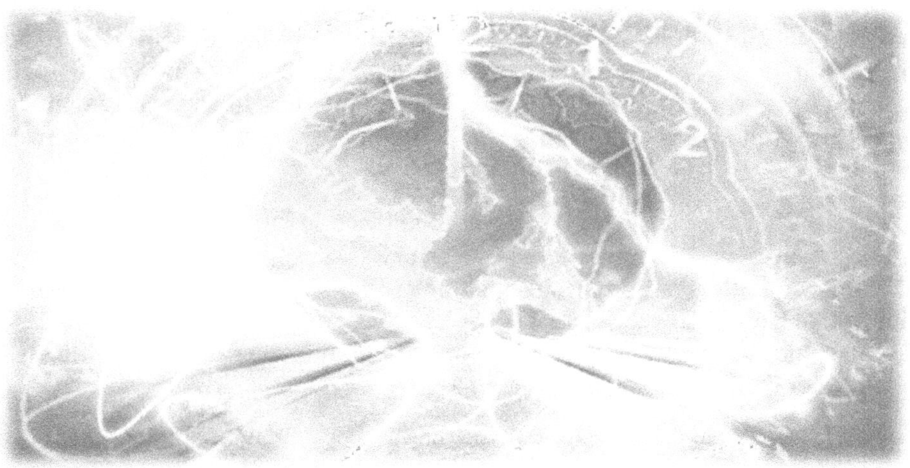

CHAPTER NINE

FALSE EVIDENCE APPEARING REAL

Gran, now the sole matriarch of the family, sat in the corner of the lounge in her eldest son's house. She was holding up well considering her youngest son had been brutally murdered by her youngest grandson. She displayed grace and dignity through all this noisy comeuppance. She bore no grudges and was prepared to allow that all that happened was for a much higher purpose than anyone here was prepared to acknowledge this day. The family grief at their unsubstantiated loss would not allow forgiveness in this family nor any wider understanding of any kind in this circumstance. They were emotionally ignorant and too close to allow real understanding. What they saw and heard at the hearing were the facts, nothing else mattered.

She was glad when the pandemonium was over. Gran was happy to return to her little island by herself and await word of the sentencing.

Before the trial, Gran would catch a glimpse of Eli and he would stare back defiantly, as if worried that she may discover something. Even if she did, there is nothing she could do about it. She had no proof. He would then kiss her on the cheek to validate his fear of betrayal.

Gran loved watching her grandsons since they were born. According to her allegiances, Eli was algorithmically designed to carry out this act of treachery since his birth. She felt there was always a darkness within him that he had to follow, she simply didn't know what it was. Everyone noticed it and would comment on it however according to Grans codes even darkness is purposefully created for some preordained purpose of perfection.

From birth Eli would constantly manifest trouble and wickedness for his family. Gran would watch how he set his older brother up constantly to take the fall for him. Then Eli would smile his supercilious smirk, knowing that gran knew. Because he knew she was not allowed to interfere in their upbringing this gave him the power he needed to continue some intensely unacceptable behaviour.

Eli would also watch her now and while struggling to maintain an innocent presence he regularly felt she was suspicious She was always skeptical? Would she do or say something? She never seemed to like him; he didn't like her either she was a witch; she always displayed preference to Liam. They would laugh and have fun together; Eli could never do that with her. Eli always felt their relationship was anxious and strained.

Weeks passed and now Eli sat before the sentencing judge for his final penalization. All the family gave their reasons why he should be put away for justice's sake. Gran watched as she saw a dark stranger had infiltrated her baby grandson's body. The grandson she knew was not present in the court room. This cold persona sat despondently with a light smile on his face. This was read by the justice system as impertinent, unremorseful, and hard-hearted.

He would serve the full 25 years without parole because he showed no repentance for his action. He callously and cold heartedly slammed an extensively long knife through his loving father, who provided his every need. He was a selfish, gold-digging brat who's only motive for killing his father was his financial gain.

As the guard pulled him away, Eli stumbled and the sentients hauled him to his feet. Hatred governed the room for most of the assembly but one old woman appeared to see through this performed façade. She was always considered weird and most didn't listen to her philosophies so she kept her opinions to herself. "It's done, finished, over," she thought.

All contenders left the court room and returned to a new form of normality. But it wasn't the life Liam's wanted to experience. He'd make plans and they'd never work out. Everything would go wrong. His plans to join his cousin disintegrated into ashes, when the family discovered the cousin got married, which was great but the newly married couple really didn't want an irrational boarder.

Months again zoomed past and Gran hadn't seen her loving Liam for quite a while so she finally managed some courage to visit him at the scene of the crime.

With a surprised look on his face, Liam opened the front door to see Gran standing in the facade unannounced. He embraced her for a long time on the front step, then apologetically allowed her to enter. He was flummoxed and flustered as he fidgeted around explaining that she should have called. He wasn't expecting visitors.

"Do you want me to leave?" she gracefully asked. "I can come back another day."

Whether it was the calmness of her voice or the reaction of her words Liam instantly calmed down, "no, it's wonderful to see your beautiful face. With all the chaos around me, your face is exactly what I need to see right now, I'm sorry." He held her again, only this time with a more welcoming embrace.

She was a strange old biddy and he loved her dearly. She saw things differently, lovingly and he needed a good dose of that at the moment. He was surrounded by adamant non-forgiving family members and friends who kept over indulging their philosophies of hatred and grief at the loss of a man none of them truly knew or liked.

The odd pair exchanged the usual social graces. Liam offered her a cup of her favourite tea; he said he had no food but he could make her a sandwich as Gran softly explained she didn't come for the beverages, but would love the tea.

Liam stated as he set the tea in front of her, "You always do that,"

She questioned to what he was inferring. "When my world is on its head, you have always had the capability of setting it up right for me again."

"Everyone has choices," was her crass reply

"I know, I try, but," jabbered her very emotionally victimised grandson.

"No one said it was easy," she reassuringly responded. She rested in comfortably in her favourite lounge and started enjoying her tea.

"How is he?" She asked very deliberately, knowing that this question would pave the way to what she really wanted to discuss with him, if he wanted to listen.

Liam sighed as he had to inform her that he found it difficult to find the courage to see him. He didn't know how to talk to him anymore. "He's not the man I knew. He's a complete stranger."

She smiled and blatantly remarked, "you have no idea how close to the truth you may be." She paused a moment to collect her thoughts.

"There were several things I'd noticed in the last few years, strange events that came out of the blue with him," Gran rationalized.

As Liam got himself a stronger drink, "like what?"

"His sudden strange inconsolable hatred for dogs in the last year or so. Where did that come from?

Liam responded that although he knew about it, he didn't see it as a concern. Gran replied, "Nothing's unimportant darling, He loved them when he was young, now he cannot stand any near him. His personality started changing from that period on. He spoke wretchedly to your father. Your father would bitch to me about it, trying to victimise me into agreeing with him."

She smirked and whispered to herself as she sipped her hot tea, "Stupid man thought I didn't know the truth about what was going on."

Liam turned and looked at Gran rather stunned and amazed at what she just said. What did she know? he thought

As if reading his mind, she responded "Oh I know more than you know. All of it my love and more." She relaxed more as if, this was the first time she would be able to vent, just a little.

"After your grandfather passed away, I became your father's first punching bag before your mother." She watched Liam's expression alter. "You didn't know that; it was to shut me up. He hated me and my philosophies. He kept me around for your grandfather's money. He didn't throw your mother out, she had to leave him. She wanted a divorce. He then took you children as revenge to stop her from having you. It was never because he loved you, he simply couldn't afford for her to have you." She sighed again, "Such a bastard. He took out a false restraining order against her. Money gets you anything. He bought judges, lawyers, the entire legal constituency. He had them all in his pocket. He was never thinking of you it was always about his wealth and money. He was never going to divide it, selfish bastard."

"That's another reason Eli lost the case. Your lawyers were bought or threatened by your father partners. He owned them all, even in his death. They had no intention of letting Eli get a lighter sentence. Too many people need him gone, he knows too much. He's safe now. But don't judge them; this is how it's all meant to be and all of them will get their own comeuppance."

"Safe?" He frowned. Gran smiled a reassuring smile.

Liam was disheartened for he hoped Gran had a more positive approach. He stood quietly with his back to Gran for he didn't want her to read his anxiety and powerlessness, and she would have.

Gran altered the dialogue, "Did you notice how Eli was almost smiling when the magistrate was handing down his sentence?"

"Yeah, they said it was contemptuous,"

"As if they'd know; this is Karmic Justice." She waited for him to turn around. She sipped her tea topping it up with some more hot tea from the pot. He turned and gave her the response everyone would to a comment like that.

"Oh, don't give me that look,' Gran justifiably responded, "it's all karmic justice, it's just we cannot condone karmic justice, there is no court for that form of justice. No one wants to understand it, but everyone wants a piece of it, and that's our problem." Gran went frustratingly quiet.

He sat beside her and displayed that he was interested. Gran continued. "That hateful person who wanted your father dead has finally got his revenge, and your father, his final punishment." Then with a strange air about her she continued. "Murder is such a long enduring path; repeated history shows this and it doesn't only concern the two participants. Look around you, this journey involves... so many people," then her sombre personality vanished as she humorously blustered, "I just want to see how it ends."

Liam laughed as Gran finished her story. He always found them mind opening and expansive. His curiosity was aroused now. True or false she always had a way of putting new spin on things that gave a person hope and Liam was looking for hope right now. An answer, true or false he didn't care, he needed something that he could possibly grasp that could help him move forward.

"I've been examining this entire situation," she continued. "Nearly everyone who knew you father or was close to him literally hated his guts. Eli just got in first. If he missed, one of the remaining adversaries would have done it sooner or later. When you match all the stories of everyone involved in this murder, we've all been synchronized to be here at this time together, but why?"

She smiled as she remembered, "The Eli we knew, was a rat bag but that's all he was. He wasn't a cold-blooded murderer until the dogs. Then his personality began to alter and he re-transformed into this new vehicle of the wretched cruelty he needed to be to do the job. He's been here before."

Liam wanted to believe but all this information was too much to absorb at this time.

Gran continued. "Our Eli wasn't in that room that day." She sipped more of her tea. "That person didn't care what verdict was handed down. That lad got what he finally wanted. This could have taken centuries to achieve. He would have had to learn to hate so intensely that he had the ability to kill up close and in cold blood. That takes time and a lot of horrible existences."

Liam listened, he uncrossed his legs, got up and bought the alcohol over to the table. He decided to settle in for the conversation. He offered Gran a glass and she happily decided to join him. This was a surprise. Liam had never taken a drink with his Gran before, and he liked the coziness.

As she sipped the drink, "your father disapproved." She sipped again, "Bloody pompous ass bastard making out the appearance of your Gran drinking would soil your poor little interpretation of what Grandmother was supposed to look like. Truth is, he was just a selfish tight asshole who didn't want to share his cheap booze."

Liam laughed. He'd never heard anyone speak of his father like that. Because of his money they spoke in awe of him and she was right, he was mean, cruel, violent and tight. He only shared when it made him look good and gave him the power to victimise. He was good at that.

Gran pondered "Eli's age is important, this occurred when he was a young boy. So, whatever happened also occurred at the same age he was when he threatened this revenge. So, he was only young." She paused and was enjoying her drink. Then excitedly she says "The other thing I noticed was the size of the weapon."

"Size of the weapon?" gasped Liam "what the fuck, do you mean? Sorry Gran," he pauses as he realises, he swore in front of the family matriarch.

She laughed as she nearly choked on her drink. "You think I've never heard that word before. I don't use it but it has never worried me. It's a word nothing more. You can say ffffff to your heart's content and it will mean nothing. It's the feeling behind the word that brings you the malcontent.Haven't you learnt that yet?" She pauses, "probably not from your father he never understood it either. You were saying"

"Oh yeah the knife;" he stopped silent. "It was a carving knife on the bench in the kitchen." he expelled with exasperation

"That's my point. If there were swords or something bigger, he probably would have used them. This was very personal. The hatred was so intense. Too intense for this petty crime. This was a bigger score to settle. This goes back centuries." She downed the last sip of drink.

"You have a lot of questions to ask him." She stretched out her glass for another. "This is good stuff"

"Don't you go getting tight now," Liam laughed, "do you eat pizza or take away I'll order us something. You can stay the night I'd like that. Haven't had a good chat like this with anyone since all this mess started, I'd like to hang onto it for a while if that's ok."

Gran smiled, "Let's do it. Let's get tight together. If I fall down just cover me with a blanket."

Liam laughed at the prospect but, "Nah, the spare room has all facilities for all types of guests. I'm sure you'll find something to accommodate including a nice bed. Just give me a minute. Do you have a favourite topping?"

"Surprise me," was her response. She got up to have a look in the spare room and was surprised at all the necessities she could use. Better than what she had. This would be ideal. She returned to the sitting room. "Impressive."

Liam smiled at her approval, "It hasn't been used for ages. Glad you like it."

Liam queried as he re-nipped both their glasses. "You think I should ask him all what stuff? You think he'll listen?"

"Oh, come on now. At least half fill it," laughed Gran. "You'll be here all night filling the bloody thing if you don't"

Liam chuckled at the new woman in front of him, "Sorry Gran I'm just not used to seeing you drink."

Patting his hand as she took her beverage, "I'll sit on this for a while instead of nipping me up all the bloody time. Yes, he needs to know what happened too. Remember at one stage he said, he couldn't remember doing it. However, the lawyers blew that out of the water with all the pre-planning that he put into it. Logically that would make sense. But what if he didn't remember *doing it*, that puts a different connotation on it for me. What if this entire incident was set up centuries ago by an old enemy of your fathers who used Eli's psyche to get revenge?"

"What are you saying a split personality or something?" Liam was thinking she's clutching at straws now.

"Yeah, that's stretching it a bit, even for me, but we don't know enough about this stuff yet. Bloody hell I want to be here when we find out." She laughed and decided to continue

"You my darling boy said you had nothing to discuss when you go to see him well ask him. Find out what provoked him really. He's the only one who can give you answers, I can't. But it would be nice to really hear his side of his story" she pondered for a minute. "But how open are you to really listening. You may not like many of the answers."

Liam deliberated for a minute rubbing his chin, there was silence as Gran was ready to listen to his questions of the possibilities. She could see all the inconsistencies in his head now starting to shuffle around like a crazy whirlwind. Liam sat back for a moment and allowed his mathematical brain to open new avenues for thought.

Gently Gran asked in a mellow tone, "How do you feel about your brother Liam, not how do you see him; how do you feel about him?"

There was an extra-long pause, then he shook his head, "I don't know" He waited for there had been a huge obstacle that had always been caught in his throat from the time he started believing that his brother did this horrendous act and this thought created a huge blockade in his relationship with his brother.

"If my friend hadn't called me to go and celebrate our great PhD success, I would have been here too. Going out was totally impromptu. I don't go out Gran. If it was for the money, he would have had to kill me too." This thought exposed an unfathomable fear all over Liam's face. "That's why I want to know more; it's also why I don't want to know more."

Gran bent forward and touched his hand, "Oh, my lovely, there is no such thing as coincidence." She smiled as she was proud to say that, "Yes, he may have had to do this, but every intricate detail had to fall in place exactly as it did for it to occur You were never meant to be here. This proves that you are far more important to him than you both realise." She paused a second as she remembered.

"All your life you have looked out for him; taken the blame for him; covered for him. You were more of a father to him than your father was. This to me says that in the past when all this happened you were unavailable to help him and your father may have seriously harmed him, and threw him to the dogs."

"Gran that's horrible," said Liam as he heard the knock at the front door. "That'll be the food."

"I'll get some plates" responded Gran.

"No plates Gran. We'll eat this out of the box," he laughed.

"Ooh, we're going commando," laughed Gran.

"Nooo Gran," he cracked up laughing at her totally unexpected remark. "No more for you," he was laughing out loud again. He hadn't done that for such a long time. This sweet little old woman had reached a part of his heart again that he thought he'd lost forever.

As they ate and continued chatting Gran revealed "This murder, this path, it's finished now; which means we're at the pinnacle of realisation. We can continue it or" …. With a huge smile on her face "let's all start again. Create a new path."

She informed Liam that he needed to live his own life the way he wanted to live it. Eli was very much a part of that life. How he treats his brother now is what will be his future path.

"What if this judgement from the world misinterprets the real balance of the universe? In other words, what if because they don't know the entire truth of centuries of murder and hatred, they got it wrong? What if real justice has now been served?

Now I don't care about them, but you my beautiful young man, how would you treat your brother then? That's my point. You and Eli have centuries of lives to share together now without the hell ordained by the horrid path of your father. Don't let his pathetic interpretation of life destroy centuries of the most fabulous future we can all live together for the rest of our lives."

"Don't let the opinions of other define you. They can only judge you from their level. echoed Liam.

"Especially when they are wrong," emphasized Gran. You never murder just for sake of murder. It takes a long time to become the murderer. Murder has a very long, long history, but once the murder has been committed, the reason for your journey has been revealed and it is finished. I believe, Eli reacted centuries ago and had to follow this murderous path. We all did, now we have the choice to continue or stop. I want to stop. Is that crazy?

She was enjoying their tete a tete, "What if this was a past transgression fulfilled? What if *You* told Eli, you'd be there for him and now you decided to abandon him? Do you want him to do that to you in your next life when you need him? Nah," she pauses as she stuffed her mouth with delicious pizza. "This is your life and your future. What if you decided to make him happy and be the best friend he ever had? What if this time you are in the position not to abandon him or lose him? What if you can fix this?

Oh, I don't mean get him out of prison for that won't happen but make sure he has a life when he gets out. Something went wrong last time. You weren't there to help him, so you followed suit. I know that because I have been watching you in this life and you over indulged him to be there always as if you were apologising. Well, be there this time. You'll feel better for it and I know he will too. This way you'll be able to always love him and that I think is more important than what the retribution being shown here."

Liam looked at Gran curiously, "You've been really thinking about this haven't you?"

Gran laughed, "you know me, I've been living this since I was born. Analysing life and finding appropriate answers, that's me Everyone saw the dark ill-will between Eli and your dad. No one but you cared. They all passed it off, but the way you always cushioned him, it always fascinated me.

Your father was the same. His sadist personality was there from birth. He didn't grow into it. It developed him. Then when he hit your mother, it was as if a fire burned in Eli and he would never forgive him. When I put that together with the perception that we and everything in the cosmos is simply data and feedback, I always wondered what Eli was telling me."

Their conversation went back and forth late into the evening as they both enjoyed the controversial topic. They laughed and chuckled at old memories of what the boys would get up to. Liam was surprised at all the things Gran saw. She missed nothing. They both retired late that night and Gran went home early the next morning, a little worse for wear but happy that her loving grandson was prepared to listen to an old fogey like her.

Liam was pleased Gran came, for today was the first day in over two years and a half year that he felt remotely happy. He didn't sleep much but his enthusiasm had peaked. He had all these new wonderful ideas because he realised, he wanted to share his life and future lives with his young brother. He put Gran into a taxi and said he would see her again soon. She giggled it off.

"No Gran, we're in this together, thank you." He gave her a big hug and kiss and let her go home. He had things to organise. First, he had to make arrangement to see his brother. Then he had to make an appointment to see his lawyer to find out the situation in regards the importing business. Then he had to search for a job in the chemistry research business. Whatever light Gran lit within him; it was blazing furiously. It released all the perfidious baggage and filled him with a new passion to enjoy life, all life.

Liam loved his feelings of empowerment. It was a little over whelming but he wanted to get a move on before it settled and went out again. He knew his father's family. Once they got hold of him, this flame would be drowned out with their intense hatred for Eli and he needed Eli very much alive and awake also.

"Let's start again."

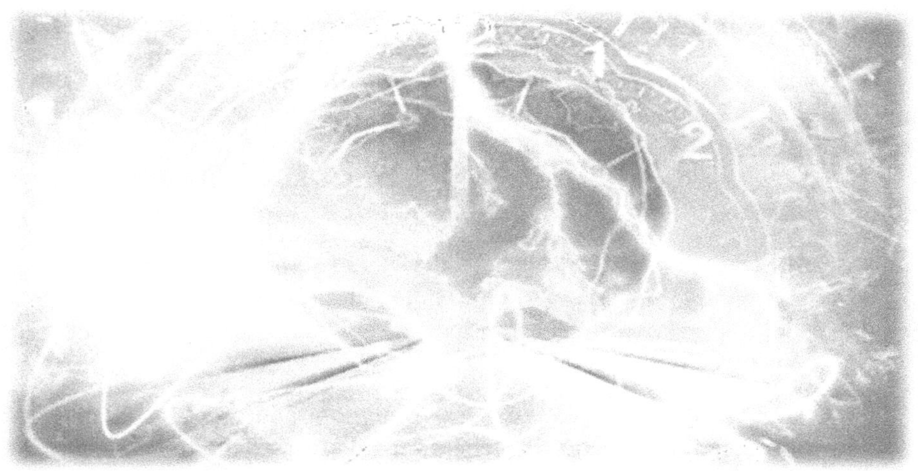

CHAPTER TEN

YOU LOSE; I'M BACK:

The new rehabilitation prison was a minimum hour and a half drive from the city. It was surrounded by a farming area out in the nothingness of the world. These male criminals were separated from society and society was separated from them. 25 years out here could either drive you insane, or turn you into a monk. The men would work in the surrounding pastures. The prison was self-sufficient to a good degree. They required as minimal contact with the outside world as possible. The prisoners weren't isolated from each other unless necessary, however, they were isolated from the world.

It could hold up to 300 prisoners maximum at one time, however, to date it was never filled to capacity. At the moment there were around 150 men inside at different levels of their sentences. There was a hospital, large kitchen and library. Internet facilities were available with all the latest modern technology. Provision was made available to all prisoners for all forms of rehabilitation. These men had to be able to display an attitude of reconciliation with the outside world before they returned.

This facility as a rehabilitation complex was proving to be very successful and was greatly supported by governments and society alike.

It was a male prison only. They were allowed conjugal visitations if they wanted it and this was highly supervised for protection of all parties. Although this was a prison for homicidal murders, most were only one-time offenders. Most offenders preferred the rehabilitation concept as opposed to incarceration or imprisonment and as a result adapted more successfully.

Liam was excited about finally seeing his brother. All his angst and grief had been erased completely thanks to his grandmother. She gave him the hope he needed to put all this emotional turmoil behind him and move on. He saw his brother as his brother again. He was no longer an angry stranger who had cast a horrendous dark cloud over everything in Liam's existence. Liam knew the situation hadn't changed. What he also realised was he had changed his perception of looking at the situation and that was what he needed.

He was no longer a victim to the circumstances. He couldn't change them; he could only alter him and Gran helped him do that. There was a lilt in his step as he stepped out of his car in the parking lot.   It was a long walk to the gate but he was ready.

Liam walked through the heavy steel door and was given a day-pass. He had to proceed to the sign in department then pass through the scanning machine. This he knew would happen. A prison guard ushered Liam to the visitation room where he sat and waited for his brother. He was expecting preventative screens and restraints of some sort but it was an open dining room set up.

Guests and prisoners alike were allowed coffee and cake if they wanted it. There were guards around the room as other visitors were present. He sat and waited for what seemed to be ages and this waiting made him anxious. The realisation of the irony of this place his brother existed in with all the restrictions, of each room bought him back to the reality of this extremely spacious but still very incarcerated world.

Finally, the shadow of the man he once knew as his brother walked through a side door and Liam stood up to greet him. Liam was warned handshakes only, no embracing or touching. He smiled at his younger brother who had dramatically changed. It had been almost two and a half years since they last touched. Eli looked drained and forlorn. The personality of his incarceration reeked out of every cell of his body; it had taken its long hard toll out on him. Eli had aged dramatically. He was no longer the sassy young teenage boy who bounced around the house with the worst sense of humour, cracking really bad jokes and manifesting outlandish practical pranks.

Eli's apprehensiveness owned his persona. Liam was the first visitor Eli had received since his imprisonment. He had no idea what to expect. He'd never been in this room before not even with his lawyer. He expected the worst. The outside world saw him in different eyes now. They put him in a box he really didn't wish to exist in. He didn't want to play victim but the situation forced it upon him.

"You look crap" was Liam's introduction greeting to his brother as he smiled

Eli wasn't impressed and scourgingly grunted, "Thanks. What do you want?" He condescendingly listened as Liam tried to break the ice.

"I want you to forgive me for not being here for you. I'm not angry with you. Oh, don't get me wrong, I was. I was really pissed. But you know that crazy thing about our family?"

Liam looked at Eli's non- enthusiastic face. "Gran"

Eli scoffed at his comment in disgust, "Is that old witch still alive. I thought the shock of me killing her baby son would have put her in a box for sure."

Liam rebutted swiftly, "Don't under estimate her. She's one of your greatest fans. Always has been. She has watched you from the beginning. The stories she tells me about you, I had totally forgotten."

"But that cow hated me," remarked a very unreceptive Eli. "She always kept company with you and ignored me. I couldn't talk to her."

"That wasn't her fault." Responded Liam defensively. "It doesn't mean she didn't watch you and she did. She would watch how you would cavort all the things to get me in trouble because you missed mum. She knew that." Liam took a deep breath and continued for this subject was veto territory. "She knew you were close to mum and she knew you missed her terribly and felt abandoned. She knew how much dad abused us and how he used your affiliations with mum to abuse you more."

"What before she fucked off and killed herself and left us to be with that bastard." In a slightly raised voice Eli roused, "Why didn't Gran do something then? Why didn't she stop him? No one did. No one could."

Liam sighed as the realisation of abuse of their youth unveiled itself from his brother's painful perspective. "Because if she stepped in, dad would have used that against you even more. She knew dad. What I didn't know was that before dad started abusing mum, he was using Gran as his punching bag. She didn't intervene, because he would have abused us more."

Eli sat back in his chair feeling less defensive, for that comment although very unsatisfactory, would have been the truth.

"Gran knew how he worked. She knew how he used his money to outcast her and that loss is what killed her. She knew all that. She also knew that by staying in your life dad would create a semi buffer and bitch about us and this is how she could see both sides of the coin. She knew dad was a huge liar, playing victim, but he would tell her what we were doing. He would tell her how you were rebelling and how you've changed. Then she would watch."

Eli sarcastically smirked, "Watch what? Is that why you're here?"

Liam sat back and relaxed more now "In a way. I've got a couple of questions to ask you."

As he said that Eli sat back, and indignantly was ready for any question he could throw at him. He was still angry and very much on guard.

"Don't be like that," Liam paused and smiled "Just things Gran saw and she believes that this is more like Karmic justice because of how it all occurred rather than outright money-orientated murder.' He paused a moment, "that's the first time I've been able to say the word."

Eli patronizingly laughed, "Oh you get used to it, believe me." Eli sat back and crossed his arms "The women's a bloody fruit cake; you do know that don't you?" exclaimed Eli.

"Maybe, but there are some irregularities. Like one, what's with your intense hatred for dogs now?"

Eli frowned at him thinking what the hell is he talking about?

"And another, why were you smiling at the handing down of the verdict?"

Eli shook his head, "Fuck what is this an interrogation. I don't even remember that day. It's a blur. I didn't know my sentence until they bought me back to the holding cell and told me that they would putting me in Burnside. But then, things changed and they bought me here instead for the next 25 years. The guard called me a smug bastard. Whatever?"

"That's what Gran said. She said the guy who killed dad was the one smiling and he was glad it was done. Final retribution, an injustice from a past life."

Now Eli was shaking his head "You believe that shit? I killed him. I killed our father. I did this; not some cockhead from a thousand years ago, I did. I'm the one who has to live with this shit, you don't."

"That's where you're wrong. We both do." pleaded Liam. "I can't live without you in my life and this shit, this Gran shit, as you call it, will help me interpret it from a different perspective."

Eli had just about had enough. He was not going to be some charity case. "You owe me nothing, I did this and I have to pay; that's it no more." He began to feel unsettled and wanted to leave.

Liam quickly responded hoping he could reach him with compassion, "You still see you as dad's murderer, I don't. I see you as my brother."

Pretending to be more logical than emotional Liam continued "Oh, I know you have to do the time because you did the crime shit but it's over finished, done; now I have more to offer. I can get passed it and move on and hopefully, so can you with me I'm not asking you to think like this but if you know this is how I think, maybe you will give me some leeway. Please, that's all I ask?"

Relentingly Eli gave a small smile and relaxed to listen to his brother's bullshit. "Fuckhead. As long as I don't have to think like you, okay. Give me what you've got. This ought to be good."

"At least you're smiling, that means something." Liam responded.

Eli giggled. It had been a long time since he even smiled. This visitation was slowly becoming more comfortable than he expected.

"Gran believes you hated dad from birth."

Eli interjected, "Don't know wasn't there but doesn't surprise me. When he belted mum, I wanted to kill him then. I hated him. What was I, five, six?"

Liam's face altered as he remembered "Nah, it was more than that and you started intensely hating him again when you started reacting to dogs about two maybe three years ago."

"That was that filthy Doberman. It was a mongrel of a thing. I hated the bloody thing, still do. Something about its filthy mouth."

Liam quickly interjected "Dad told Gran you started rebelling then."

"Rebelling?" Eli mocked "Son of a bitch." He shook his head back and forth, "He wanted me to run his filthy business." He couldn't believe what he was about to reveal to his brother. "And I didn't. He and his crooked cronies were into some deep shit and I was getting a Ph.D. in business acumen and he didn't give a fuck about any of the legalities, and I was rebelling." Eli scoffed at the indignant slur.

Eli sat upright, "My eyes were being opened to the felonious operations he would carry out to get what he wanted illegally and he wanted me to continue this…. this illicit multi-million dollar smuggling operation because he had gotten away with it for years and the Govt. hadn't caught him yet." He sat back with his arms crossed and breathed a sigh of disgust.

"I lost all respect for that prick years ago. Yeah, I hated him more than ever before. Then when he threatened to wipe me out because I wouldn't do it his way that was the last straw. I had to pass my studies to totally ignore everything I had ever learnt, so I could become as big a degenerate as him, because he knew better. It was a joke. And here's the biggest joke of all.

If he got caught, it wouldn't have been him that went down, it would have been me. That bastard would have let me hang."

Liam reacted, "Yeah, but that's no reason to kill him." Then he pensively stated, "Well at least now I know it wasn't some crime of greedy passion."

"I wouldn't know" came the despondent rebuttal.

"Same age, same person, karmic restitution. He did this to you in a past life and now you are redeeming yourself," echoed Liam

Eli started shaking his head with a grin. "You're so fucked."

"The passion of hatred at the scene of the crime doesn't match the crime. The knife's too big." declared Liam.

"That's your educated opinion Sherlock?" reacted Eli

"If there was a bigger knife you would have probably used it, like a sword." Liam paused and watched Eli's curious reaction.

Eli burst into laughter. "That's funny, I couldn't find his Japanese swords" He laughed to himself. Liam was shocked at that revelation. Eli saw his reaction and decided to explain. "I was going to make out someone was stealing them and got caught. You do know that if you were home, you would have been in the firing line too. You do know that," he stated with a cocky presence.

"That's the other thing. I wasn't there. I was never meant to be there." He paused to see Eli's reaction.

"That's what I couldn't get passed either. But I was never meant to be there. There are no mistakes or coincidences, I no longer believe in them. You don't have to answer but I want to ask you something really weird, so don't take this the wrong way."

Eli sniggered, "Oh, you mean this hasn't been weird enough? You should be in here. You'd fit right in."

Liam carried on regardless. "Ah there it is; that sarcastic wit, how I've missed it." he paused and snidely continued. "When you did the act, was it you? Or did it feel like someone else, because this passion of hatred was too intense for someone like you."

Eli looked at him in astonishment. "Someone like me?" He stopped still "I haven't been someone like me for years." He exhaled heavily, "I don't know, I don't know what I was thinking at the time. Wow you two must have had a great whinge session about me. The topic of the month."

"No, you've got it wrong." Then Liam recalled with a smile "We drank a bottle of scotch and had pizza and she stayed overnight and we had a freaking ball and the old lady swears like a bloody trooper. She made me laugh again. She made me see a light. She showed me how this thing was imprisoning me and I had a choice." Liam concluded with determination, "I could let it bury me or I could get on with my life my way, and my dear brother as much as you hate the idea, you are very much a part of that life."

Eli vindicated "I don't need your help. I'm fine. You get on with your life. You're better off forgetting about me and living your own life."

"Wow that was a pitiful excuse for a vicitmising party if ever I saw one. You sound like the misery family. I've had enough of them too. I don't do 'But Zones' anymore."

Eli laughed, "Damn. I haven't heard that for years. That was one of her favourites. What was the rest of it? I don't kiss butt either" He nodded his head.

"You're stuck with me Eli." Liam pointed his finger at his brother and with a huge grin on his face, "You lose."

"They're telling me I have to go now but next week I want to come and see you again. Is that okay? Apparently, I have to ask you if you will give me more time. I'd like that, can I stay longer next time, please?"

Eli sighed but had to smile, and as he nodded, "Yeah I would actually like that too. Gran to a min though," he pleaded with a heavy frown on his face, "This turned out better than I expected. I have to admit I had no idea what was going to happen here, and I wasn't very optimistic. This was sorta nice, thank you," he paused as he remembered," There is another rule too. After about a month if we prove to be trust worthy they let us get closer. I'd like that too."

"Now there's my brother. Me too. I will really do my best to get them to trust us both. You really are stuck with me now. See you next week."

Liam stood up and took his brothers' hand in his and lingered for a while. He smiled and gave it one good last shake and departed, turning back and waving.

Both Liam and Eli walked out of the room different men. Lighter happier and ready to start again.

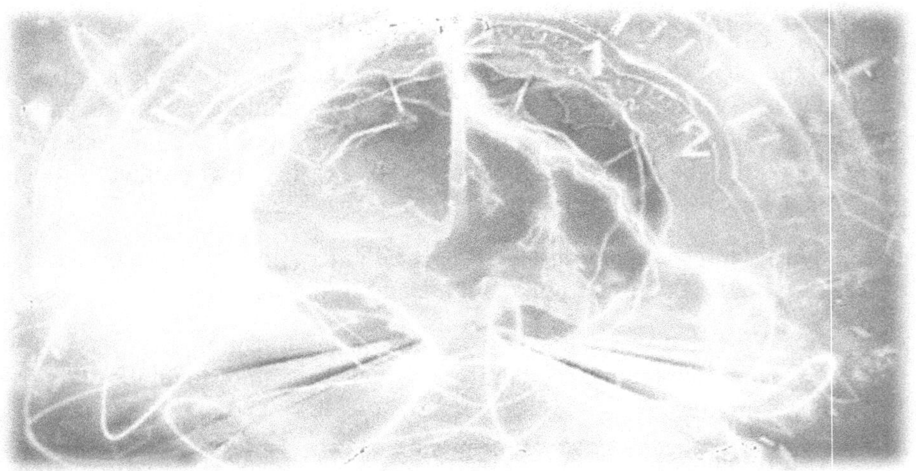

CHAPTER ELEVEN

DREAM BIGGER

Was Gran right? Is it possible that the murder was the end of the story? Could they now really start again? Neither had any idea where this path would lead but a clean slate for both of them would be ideal. 'We could pave a way to a much better path, well, better than the one we had been forced to travel, thought Liam.'

The following week couldn't pass fast enough, for Liam was the happiest he had ever been for many years. For the first time in his life, he wasn't walking on egg shells trying to please other people. He stayed as far away from his father's family as he could and would phone Gran and give her progress reports on how happy he was. Gran commented,

"Now my little man is writing his own music instead of playing everybody else's songs."

Gran was elated for she knew if her boys could harness the key to their real happiness, both boys would, regardless of where they were and had been; they could still excel in life and achieve all their dreams and more. But what would she know she was the family fruitcake, an old-time witch?

Three offers came in for positions of a career for Liam, and there was one for an international company which he dearly wanted to investigate.

Come Sunday Liam was excited about seeing his brother again for he had some excellent proposals to discuss with him. He was already seated when Eli arrived and he too looked far healthier than he did the previous week.

Eli now had a slight bounce in his step. They shook hands and sat quietly facing each other and both began talking at once. They laughed and allowed the other to speak first.

Liam said "You first,"

"I think this place is driving me mad." Eli responded as Liam looked concerned. "I've had a lot of time to think over the last few years and last week with all the crap you bought in, it all started coming back, but differently this time. Instead of trying to erase it, I thought about it. Strangely enough a lot of it now sort of registers more cos I'm not in the middle of it."

Liam moved in closer as he laughed. "Oh great, you were supposed to be the sensible one." They began to speak more quietly.

A sombre look donned Eli's face as he slowly proceeded, "You started this shit, so are you prepared to listen," Eli laughed as Liam nodded. "You said its finished, over, done. I remembered the old witch would say, when the catastrophe hits its only telling why you are there. Now you get to start again." he smiled at his reminiscence. "Didn't know I was listening did you," Eli smirked. "I know I did it, I remember the scene. It haunts me every night. I don't wake up in the horrors anymore, but the vision is always there. I remember being afraid of returning home that night and finding him, as if it may have been a dream. But it was real and surreal at the same time."

Liam encouraged him to continue, "I don't remember being in court for the verdict. I remember falling and some men pulling me up but before that there's nothing. I know people were talking horribly about me but I didn't hear what they were saying.

I don't remember smiling. I don't remember the magistrate. I only remember that night the guard told me I got 25 years. And then he called me *a smug bastard* and I wondered what I did to deserve that. I thought he was going to kill me." Eli paused and breathed heavily as if grateful to get that weight off his chest.

With a smile of disbelief, "What if the old witch is right? How do you get out of messes like these if it is a thing from some past but you have to re-live it anyway?" He shuffled in his seat as he queried, "Where is the old bugger when you need her?" He smiled and confessed, "Who'd a thought that she'd be the one who has given me some sort of hope or reprieve, and that's something I never expected to ever have again. Don't tell her I said that, but thank her for not giving up on me will ya, please. I feel a lot of his family wants me dead cos I killed the mighty maestro." Eli whispered as he sat in disgust, as his head filled with the memories of just how great an orchestrator his lying father was.

Liam touched Eli's fingertips, then he held his hand up to the guard indicating it was okay. He sat in silence and smiled at his brother. "Let's start again. I've got some really good ideas but I'd genuinely appreciate your input?"

Eli looked at him questioningly, raising his arms and swinging around indicating, "do you know where I am?"

Liam shrugged it off like a little kid and enthusiastically continued. "I checked it out and you can study in this facility."

Eli's ears pricked and he listened with humorous curiosity.

"Well, would you be interested in finishing your business degrees in here and running the importing business with me and I'll do whatever you say," Liam pleaded

Eli gasped at the suggestion. "No one would let me take over any business let alone my father's, whom I murdered in case you forgot."

"It's my business now," stressed Liam, "and I have no idea how to run it." He pauses to breath. "This way I can continue what I love to do and I've been offered a great position and I'd love to take it but I can't leave the business in the hands of those crooked accountants that are running it now. They'll either bleed us dry or have us all put in jail."

Eli laughed "I'd take the latter."

"You could use the business as your practical, your hands-on experience." Eli covered his mouth with his hand and breathed through his fingers making a farting sound like a child. "You missed the lawyers, dad owned them, they're shoddy too" He remarked. Then he leant forward in his chair and thought for a while,

"That could be sooo dangerous," he mumbled through his hand.

"We have to start somewhere. Create our own life. Are you're in?" questioned Liam with high hopes.

"Are you fucking kidding me," exclaimed Eli. "This is the most ridiculous idea you have ever come up with in your entire life, of course I'm in. Someone has to watch your back; but they won't let you do it." Eli warned as Liam laughed with anticipation.

Eli paused awhile, then a very stern appearance beheld his entire body and he patronizingly commented, "So, you know all there is to know about dad's business?" Eli hesitantly asked as he saw an apprehensive gaze on Liam's face, "I didn't think so."

Eli prepared himself to reveal a side of this parent Liam may not want to know about. "When I say dad was in with some very dangerous people, I don't think he did drugs but, he was a mercenary and a lot of the stuff he bought was for," he paused for a while, "let's say the darker side of the black market. He had cops, judges, lawyer's accountants and the merchants all in his pocket. Then he had the legal facade import business which was the cover up, but it never was where he made his wealth. He didn't know how to do importing to make a profit."

"I can do the imports and make a huge profit, there's no problem there and I would do a bloody good job, but that other shit," he sat a minute, "nah…. I'm not into that and I have no idea how you would escape it alive unless you sell it to them…. dead."

Totally disregarding everything Eli just said, Liam continued, "How long would it take to finish your degree in here?" he questioned.

Eli smugly laughed, "You're serious about this aren't you? You didn't hear a word I said?" he responded in disbelief and concern, slowly he reiterated word for word, "Dad's family will crucify you. They'll think you were in on the murder to get the business as well. They are the most indignant group of hypocrites that ever existed. They'll fight you. They'll kill you." Frustratingly Eli threw up his arms, "Why are you doing this anyway? The entire thing is utterly ridiculous?"

"You getting cold feet." stated Liam as he sat back in his seat feeling very confident that his stupid plan was the best he had ever had. "You didn't answer my question and if we are going to do this we need to move fast before they do get wind of it." Now Liam sat with a surly business look on his face.

Eli shook his head and shrugged his shoulders then out of frustration, "a year maybe eighteen months more or less, I don't know."

"Would you do it? Do you want to do it?"

Eli smirked, "Liam, I always wanted to sail. I never wanted any of this shit." Dad always said I was a loser throwing my life away on fanciful dreams. He always made me feel guilty because I didn't want his mafia lifestyle." Throwing his arms up in the air

"Yeah, the ungrateful loser son who didn't want his father's crooked import business." He wiped his eyes in frustration. "I couldn't win"

"Okay we'll change the subject. How has your week been?"

With the pressure off for the next two hours they talked small talk about how the prison works and where everything is. How he works in the fields and does his share of cleaning and tiding. By the time the visit was over Liam was aware of all the comings and goings of the prison and how remarkable the system really was.

They talked about Liam's job proposal and where it would take him. And then it was time to leave.

"I'll call you" said Eli as Liam began walking away.

"You can do that; you would do that?" questioned Liam. "I tell you what, if I have visitors, as in family, I'll make out you're someone else. Okay. As you said we have to be careful."

Both boys were saddened at the ending of the visit for their time together was warmly healing for both of them. "It's really good seeing you Eli, I really mean it. See you next week. Maybe I'll have a better idea."

As Liam walked away, he looked back to wave but Eli was being escorted to his room with guards at his side. The reality again hit home.

Liam feeling more determined mumbled to himself. "You're stuck with me kid. We're going to find our dream. You lose, we are starting again," He bit his bottom lip as he walked through the prison door.

On the Wednesday night Liam received a phone call from a strange number. He answered his mobile. "Three years; it will take me three years to get the degree I want. I will have a full business Ph.D. and all the creds you need for a highly run brilliant import business with legal Govt. support. We can work South-East Asia, incorporating India Vietnam, and all the little countries. I will not use slave labour. And it will all be above board. Here's the buzz, but don't get your hopes up. If I show true potential and remorse, and I am sort of sad that I did it. It may give me some credit points. I may not get out early but I won't be kept in either."

"Eli, that's fantastic, I don't know what to say. Let's do this then. I'll see you on Sunday"

"You go for that job too. You deserve it" responded Eli in a gentle loving voice. "I'll see you on Sunday. And yeah, sell the business. We'll do what the old witch says, we'll start from scratch, losing dad's name. We'll create ours. I think that could work.

Another thing, you can't get the books audited because they are cooked so you'll have to get them to give you a good offer. They won't of course they'll try desperately to rip you off but I'm thinking between 30 and 50 million. They'll talk you down to 10-15. Your choice whether you want to take it; however," he pauses a minute "you will need some good capital to start buying and selling in a new market again. We'll talk more about that on Sunday. I've got to go now. Night." Then he hung up.

Liam's head was all agog. Everything was altering so fast. He saw the end product but had no idea how he was going to get there. He needed another night with Gran. She owned a resort; she could talk this business stuff. His face lit up with a smile just at the thought of seeing her again. "Yeah, Gran we need another 'Partee' night."

Liam realised how small his world was also. His business partner was his grandmother. However, after listening to Eli, this subject was extremely sensitive. He knew he could trust Gran, unlike Eli's friends in the court room. He trusted them and they all hung him out to dry.

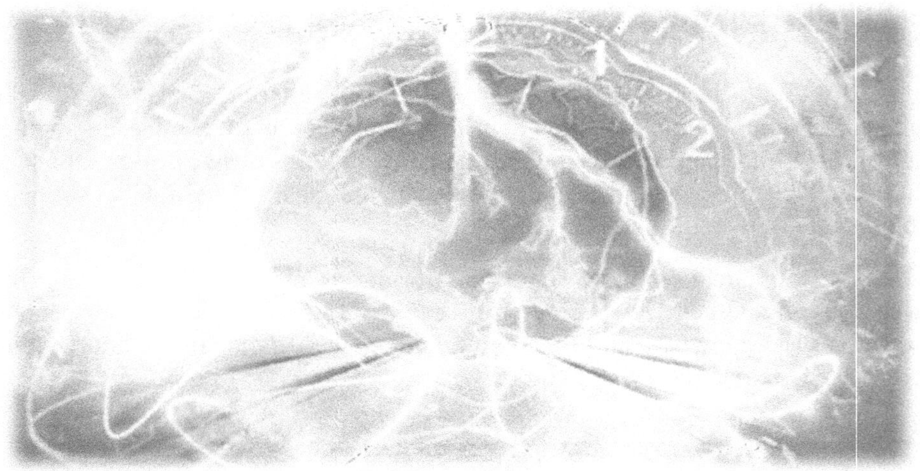

CHAPTER TWELVE

UNUSUAL BUSINESS

Liam checked that the alcohol cabinet was full and this time he bought the really smooth expensive brand. For some strange reason that seemed to be important at this time.

He arranged good pizza again and this time he prepared a limo to deliver his lovely Gran. 'That'll make the others around her sit up and look'.

Gran was unaware that this "partee night" was also an imitation board meeting.

Both did some catchup and then this time Liam got down to business. Liam didn't know how much Gran knew about her son's business. He was very wary about letting her know that her son's business was more than the importing business.

She informed him she knew what her son was up to long before Liam was born. She was amazed the government hadn't subpoenaed his records. "No one makes that much money on imports unless they own the country."

Liam mentioned his idea and stated that all he and Eli wanted was the importing business. The merchandising business, as they called it, his father's associates could keep.

"Oh, you mean your uncle's business?" confirmed Gran. She looked at Liam's amazed gaze. "Why don't you just walk away? Let them have the lot and start up your own importing business with Eli."

"I tried that two years ago and uncle basically said it would be unwise. I had inherited it and none of the associates had enough to buy me out and it was better to keep it going and the associates would take care of most of it any way. I believed them."

"Then you don't know about your dear darling uncle?" she re-questioned. "He and your father were thick as thieves. Forgive the pun,' she laughed at her impromptu gag.

"Are you naïve about business or just your father's business?" Gran stared at him in amazement. "How can you run a business for two years and not know who now sits in the chairman's seat when your back is turned?" She was stunned at how much her eldest son had kept Liam in the dark. Then she sighed as she realised, the company needed Liam there as their patsy, nice clean-cut boy, their scapegoat, she was not impressed.

"There may a couple of ways to handle this. What if you go to your uncle again; act as if you don't know he is in cahoots with the business. You're in agreement with him. Ask him to help you find out who to ask for you to buy the import business from. Give him a price to deal with and he'll get back to you." She smiled at her genius. "He'll get back to you so fast. He doesn't want the import business he wants the black marketing but he's not clever like your dad. Your dad knew the benefits of the importing business. It kept his books balanced."

Liam's ears pricked as he listened to his grandma explain his father's business. Grandma realised she may have said too much. She sipped her scotch "mm nice drop."

"Only the best." He automatically responded and wondered where that comment came from.

"You were saying dear?" Grandma asked.

Liam started laughing out loud as he commented "you never cease to amaze me. How do you know all this?"

Then Gran realised she had already let the cat out of the bag so reluctantly continued. "Actually, that may not be a good idea after all," she pondered awhile longer. 'If you are their patsy and your uncle suspects even in the smallest way that you know anything…. no that's not a good idea at all. Too many lives at stake."

Gran sipped on her drink while Liam made small talk but she was concentrating far harder on another plan. While she was contemplating, the pizzas arrived.

"Got it." She sprang up in her seat and began explaining the simplest plan. "It has to be simple, because by now they know you know nothing about business so your innocence and ignorance is going to be our weapon of choice."

Liam was slighted by her comment and wasn't quite sure what she meant. "Oh, don't go and get all huffy," she exclaimed in her defense "they know sweet bugger all about your chemistry set either."

"His lawyers, you approach your father's lawyers. You tell him your main objective is be a sole owner of your own import business. You want to buy the import business from your fathers' partners and you don't know who they are."

"I was thinking like them. That business is such a strategic mess you have to scratch and claw to find daylight. Think like a woman and it is easy." She sat back, sipped her drink and smiled at her brilliance. "That's it, simple."

"But Eli said they're crooked," stressed Liam.

"Crooked, scmooked, who cares, I'm planning on it?" responded Gran. "You just want the importing business. You agree, you inherited it and you want to maintain it, but it's too big for you, you want to make it smaller; one that you can handle. Keep it simple, no reasons, or excuses. We don't want them knowing that you know more than you should. You loved your dad, you trusted your dad, you're doing this for your dad, but you are not as smart in business as your dad, they will know that. Use all that smaltzy stuff. They'll want a mint so you make an offer."

"Eli said about 15 to 20." Liam refilled their glasses. "Maybe, but I think they'll want more, however, in saying that, to get you off their back and have the entire business outright, they may consider something close to that. So, do you have the cash?"

"I can get it." he handed Gran her glass. She smiled an unusual smile like the Cheshire cat that caught the mouse. "Cutting your uncle out, he's going to be pissed; but he never told you he was a partner in the business. So, when you see the lawyer tell him you don't know any of the associates and that's why you came to him. You can only try, but be careful the less info you reveal the safer you'll be. I know someone I'll talk to him. Now where's some food?"

They both sat back ready to enjoy their night. They enjoyed the finger food and put more of their plan into action. Liam felt he had family again. He enjoyed her company and was pleased he took her advice for now he has his brother back too, not quite the way one would call a happy family but it was his. Then in exasperation and shock, "My uncle's a crook too?"

"God love you," she cackled. "You really have no idea do you, dear." She couldn't stop laughing, "oh lord, your father was much worse."

Liam started venting about his realisation of his hibernated world. Poor Eli took the brunt of all this abuse because he knew. "Is that's why his lawyers deliberately lost Eli's case, they wanted him out of sight. Have I jeopardised his safety?" Liam began to stress.

"Oh, he'll be fine, trust me," smiled Gran as she gobbled more food. "I'm going back to the resort for a few days," she stated quickly changing the subject. Liam smiled as he remembered many a summer spent at her summer island resort. His mum, Eli and he has the best of times there.

Gran stayed the night again for now she was used to her small ensuite guest accommodation and toddled off as soon as she was tired. They had another entertaining night and many new constructive ideas were put in place.

 This was not the relationship Gran expected with her grandsons. She wasn't complaining and they were starting again, but everyone around her saw her as a dithering old fool and she was ignored and neglected and this façade gave her considerable advantage. Being in the wrong place at the wrong time. Being the stupid old battle axe, she was simply lost. Now if her eldest son finds out she was not quite so senile and she knows a little more than she should, it could create a small problem.

Gran went home the next day and Liam set about making arrangements to see the family bank and business lawyers. He wanted to have it all either in the process or finalised before the end of the month. He wanted to have a good progress report for Eli. Liam wanted Eli to want to work with him. Listening to Gran, she was right. Chemistry, anatomy, physics these subjects Liam knew but running a business being a boss in industry, he was out of his league. He thought he was doing fine, but now realises just how ignorant he must have appeared.

His father's family would have also seen how inadequate he was. They would have all known how inexperienced he was. 'I was their front boy, and if anything did go wrong, I would have been the one to take the fall, just like Eli.'

Now he felt wretched at his stupidity. He began to question why he was doing all this in the first place. Why do I want this bloody business? Eli's right it is the most ridiculous idea anybody has ever had. I've got my chemistry degree. I've got that international job. I don't need any of this crap.

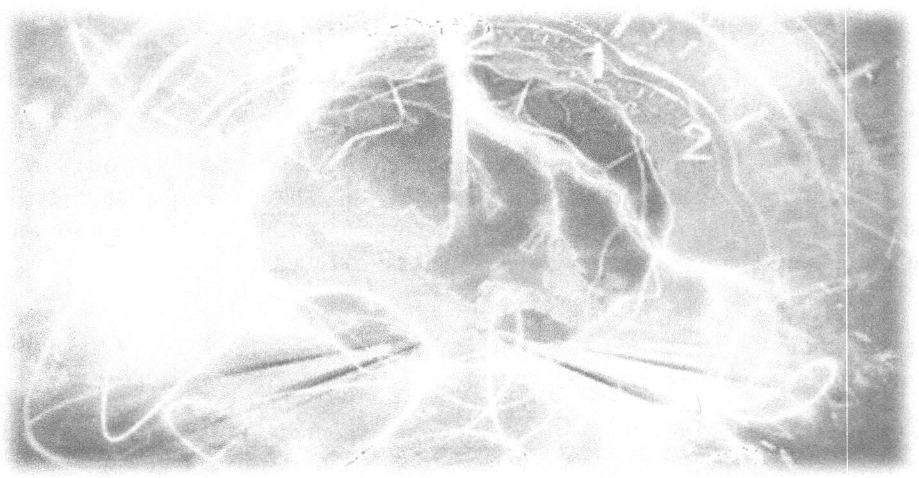

CHAPTER THIRTEEN

BALANCING THE SCALES

Sunday came and Liam went to see Eli again however, many things had altered. Eli had applied for a university degree through the prison system and within days he was also moved to a more private area away from the newer more dangerous criminals and guards. "It was as if he had a guardian angel looking after him," he laughed. All this enthusiasm and eagerness to be a success shone through Eli forcing Liam stopped feeling sorry for himself. Liam remembered why he was doing it. The smile on Eli's face said it all.

He informed Eli of a couple of plans to buy the business outright from the partners through the lawyer.

Eli smirked "partners, really?" then he pondered as he realised the naivety of the plan and the innocence of his brother, and agreed, it could work. "This way the partners…...can actually keep their business and maintain another import business under their uncle's name."

"You know about our uncle?" rebuffed Liam. He shook his head in disgust. He through his hands up into the air and exclaimed, "I didn't even know about dad."

"I could ask how the hell you didn't know or suspect, but then I think he deliberately kept it all from you as well. The narcissistic bastard saw you as sick, a weakling. He couldn't have a wimp running his dynamic enterprise." explained Eli. "He hated how clever you were. I'd love it when you'd speak and he didn't understand what you were talking about, but I did."

Eli started raucously laughing and Liam soon joined in. The realisation that they all lived under the same roof but in completely different worlds was now quite humorous. Then Liam had to ask "how many others in our family are in this underground black-market fiasco?"

Eli thought for a moment and started tallying them up, "Your cousin overseas, your aunt, she's good with legers and taxes, all of them actually. That's why dad got pissed when I told him I wanted no part of his shoddy lifestyle. He was more than happy to inform me that his underground way of life also paid for my lifestyle. He was more than happy to tell me I now owed him. I owed him for my car, my education, my friends and relatives, my social life, they were all a part of it. He owned everyone and that was his legacy for me. He wanted me to head his Mediterranean mafia.

All I wanted was the same leverage. I wanted to hurt him, then return and have him indebted to me, but it all went sideways. I remember his eyes, that's all. Dark, empty, cold like looking into the pits of hell. That's it, now this. I do remember them saying, 'all I wanted was his money,' and thinking that was the last thing I wanted of his." Eli smiled, for now it was almost 34 months since that fateful night. "My life has been a blur since then."

Liam listened for this was the first time Eli spoke about that night and now he discovered it wasn't premeditated murder at all. It was premeditated but to harm not kill. They could get another trial he could get out. Liam was getting hopeful.

Eli shook his head. "My choice, no. If I survive in here, I'll be lucky, but I won't survive out there." Eli was adamant, "clutching at straws." He paused for a moment. "Intent to harm, intent to kill, neither should have been on the plate."

Eli realised he now sounded like Gran. Who would have thought that her ramblings would have rubbed off on him? But one of her philosophies did ring true to him. The mirror concepts. When you look at another, they mirror you. "When I looked into dad's eyes, I felt his intense hatred pulse through my blood as well. I'd become that cold hearted bastard's hatred…. That's who killed him, and I don't know if I can control that?"

Their time together was extended now and they were allowed closer contact. Eli found himself understanding some of Grans more whacky concepts and started asking questions for Liam to quiz the old girl on. He too was starting to feel a family bond with the three of them, better than the bond of what he had. She may be whacky, but she was far from dangerous and she gave a damn.

Liam shared, "Gran and I have had some doozy conversations on all this since dad's death. She believes the hatred in this crime was personal. She claims he was such a bastard as a kid, that if you didn't nick him first, he actually had a line up." Liam laughed as he revealed. "She says he was born an ass and he has harmed and hurt so many people over the years and more than likely over the centuries.

And the repetition thing, it may also have something to do with ships and sailing and imports, because you love to sail and his business needs sailing So, you were nineteen and, on a ship, he was on land in the port. He would have been crooked then too. Same time, same age, same circumstances, same impact, but karmic, opposite and equal value. See I've solved it." Liam laughed as he unfolded a magical tale of mystery and adventure gone wrong.

You said you felt imprisoned by dad's desires for you, maybe he threw you in prison. What ever happened then is repeating itself now only this time it's opposite and equal and you get to be executioner, justice served, start again."

Eli frowned at such a harsh word, he didn't mean to kill him, it just turned out that way. He had to admit it was a fascinating tale though. Then he burst out with laughter. "Oh, you've got to be kidding me. Your exterior world reveals your past life. Is that what this is all about?" He laughed at the hilarity of the coincidences surrounding him.

"Add this to your story. You're not going to believe this?" he paused and pondered in disbelief himself as all the memories of the information of his father's business, started flooding through.

"Apparently before we were born, there used to be a black marketeer maverick who undercut all the buyers about 30-35 years ago and he was the best in the business. They called him the Pirate." They both started laughing. "Dad could never find him. He wanted him to go into business with him. The Pirate vanishes; however, the pirating continued and still continues today. Whoever this guy is, he picks the best then resells it to other black marketeers. They still do well but no one knows who he is or where he comes from. All above board, just underhanded and smarter than all the rest.

Eli warily warned Liam, "We may need to watch him also. He will know about us that's for sure. I'd forgotten about him. I sort of admired him. I always felt if I was going to be in the black market, he'd be the guy I'd want to be." He smiled as he reminisced over the joys of sailing. "I'd make a great Pirate," he guffawed. His brother laughed as he prepared to leave.

"I get two conjugal calls a week now. I don't know if it's a time thing or an upgrade thing but life is changing around here for me, for the better. Keeps going at this rate, I'll soon be guard," then he shook his head.

That week Liam worked on the plan to buy the business and Eli was due to meet the prison board to see what courses he needed to apply and study for to get his degree. It was to be a busy but motivating constructive period for both of them.

Both boys sat up at night in their rooms writing up their plans and agendas to present to their individual boards. By morning Liam had a solid proposal for the import business and Eli had his business marketing plan ready to present the prison board for his application for a prison University course.

Both boys were ushered by two flanked escorts to their specific rooms where a board of individuals were waiting. Both tables held five people and both boys were seated on the opposite sides of their tables.

Both boys placed their proposals on the tables and presented them to their individual boards. Both boards distributed the proposals to each person at the table who then proceeded to read the proposals.

Within ninety minutes Liam came out of the board room jumping and pumping the air with glee. His proposal had been accepted. 22 grand was the settled agreement price and they wanted it within thirty days. All paperwork was signed in duplicate and triplicate and everyone was happy. The boys could keep their father's business name and or parts thereof, if they wanted it. The board was prepared to dissolve all affiliated associations with the importing business belonging to their father. Hands were shaken, greetings were given, and Liam left never to see any of them again. The bank would takecare of the financials, all was done. It was almost too easy. Now the rest was up to Eli.

Eli sat in front of the prison board chairman and four other people. He started introducing himself and they asked him to be quiet while they read his proposal. The chairman concurred with the group that the proposal was exceptional, and showed enormous potential. One by one they started asking questions in reference to his ability to carry out the application to the fullest. His results for his last degree showed poor acumen, however this proposal demonstrated and acute business knowledge.

Holding the proposal in his hands the chairman stated, "This is good. It's original and it definitely has enormous potential, but," he paused a moment, "what I need to know why you wish to pursue the same field of study that you've already shown mediocre interest in. You have to understand, if the only reason you're doing this is to fill in time, then stop wasting ours. Give me something to hold onto."

Eli dropped his head "It's personal"

"It may be all you have son." responded the chairman staring him directly in the eyes. Eli straightened himself up and began to speak personally. This was not his forte but for Liam he would try. "I have a brother."

"Liam your partner in this venture," interrupted the head guard on the end of the table. He turned to the others and stated. "He is a regular visitor."

The members added this information to their assessment.

"My dad was not a nice person. But my brother didn't know that and my brother always came back for me through thick and thin. He didn't do it to get even with dad. He did it for me. I didn't know that till recently. Even now he is the only one who always comes to visit. He's always there for me." he sighed as small tears welled in his eyes. "When it comes to business though, the man is a total fruit, he knows nothing. Put him in front of a chemistry set and he's Mister Curie, put a ledger or bank book in front of him and he's a total buffoon, he has no idea how to interpret it, but I do." He took a breath.

We, together we, can do this. I can show him how. Then when I do finally get out, we can continue our lives as normal as we can. I can do this for him. I know it's smultzy but, that's all I got. That's why I doing it."

"Smultzy?" questioned the chairman.

"It's a Grandma thing" Eli responded as he shrugged his shoulder

The chairman stood up. He was tall and tough. Not a person you would want to tackle with. Waving Eli's proposal in front of him, "smultzy," he smiled, "that might just get you across the line."

The guards were buzzed to return him to his room, while the members left by a side door ushered by the head guard. The rest of the board were hesitant but they knew the chairman had a plan in mind and they needed clarification before they passed their vote. They weren't going to vote in favour unless it was a sure thing. He went to his side desk and pulled out the application papers. "Three years," he whispered. He then called his assistant and asked for another application to be bought into the office. "Have a drink folks, behind the bar, 'Only the best."

He waited for his female assistant to arrive with the papers he asked for. "Four years," he whispered to himself. While his associates were sampling his best scotch, he made a quick phone call. The members started asking questions. "Who and what are you doing?"

"Possibilities people possibilities," was his enthusiastic reply.

He spoke on his mobile for 3 minutes then he hung up. He poured himself a drink and sat in his lounge feeling very confident and sure of himself. The members could see a plan ticking over in his head.

"What are you up to" asked the president of the rehabilitation centres spokesman? "Money, lady and gentlemen, money," as he raised his glass in a toast.

"We can put this lad through some university course and achieve nothing. He'll get his degrees and maybe work later in life with his brother or we can make a difference and give him a University Apprenticeship."

The board listened to his innovative proposal for they wanted to know how his proposal bought in the money.

These apprenticeships can be sponsored by private and government alike. He has to do four years minimum. All books and funds are constantly audited by government and we get ongoing grants to continue them with other prisoners. Don't you see? This is the opportunity we've been looking for. To become the best rehabilitation prison in the state we have to be able to produce the best rehabilitation results. We are not only rehabilitating prisoners; we are giving them a better life to return to; that's rehabilitation.

And successful rehabilitation programs mean money folks, money. We will no longer have to struggle from some piss ant government official who suddenly doesn't want to play with us any more so they cut our funds. This is the real reason we call these complexes rehabilitation centre. So, lets rehabilitate, folks."

The board members started debating among themselves, agreeing and disagreeing to the possibility of having more security.

The chairman asked the centres president. "We need to ask him more questions. We need another interview tomorrow; can you arrange that? He nodded.

"This boy has changed." The others tweaked and started to listen. "When he arrived here, he was an iron lung. How old was he? Nineteen, twenty?" He questioned the guard. "He looked like a ninety-year-old man in a boy's body. Today, he had a lilt in his step and light in his eyes. This lad has been given hope, and I want to harness that."

The Head Guard interrupted, "He and his brother have a great time when they are together. They obey the rules, but they do laugh a lot."

"You find that annoying?" questioned the female psychologist.

"No, unusual," he responded. "None of the others really even smile."

The chairman stood at the window overlooking his caged protégées, "Loving someone is not always enough. You have to want it for yourself as well. I need to know if he has that. You're saying the love of his brother may be enough; but that edge; him wanting it too; I want that. I want that hope I saw in him today to be for him, not his brother."

The chairman waited awhile and then with a determined expression "If we can do this; if we can make him a success, make them a success, we've got this in the bag, for every prisoner who comes through here, but he needs to want it more than we do."

He raised his glass in the air, "Cheer's folks. Best idea we had yet." he laughed as the other raised their glasses and agreed.

"How do you know about the grants?" asked the female psychologist and third member of the board.

"Friends in high places," he smirked as he tipped his glass. "That was my phone call. Had a meeting with some colleagues several weeks ago and the concept of using money to create training programs of work and business for the prisoners while in prison was one of the topics. I liked some the ideas but never put it on our agenda until this lad started saying he would work for his brother. That's why he has to be a success. That why we have to assist him in being a huge success. The possibilities are endless." He stood up.

"Let me know the time for the interview tomorrow and I'll be back. I have another meeting now. Let yourselves out. Lock the door after you. Thank you, lady and gents". He bowed and tipped his head as he left the room.

When the chairman returned the next morning, he was theoretically prepared and determined for success. He organised the interrogating interview room to be set up. He wanted associates to listen in the adjoining room as he wanted private access on the behavioural habits of his prisoner by the psychologist. He needed to know whether the kid was worthy and was telling the truth or lying.

The chairman's government apprentice proposal was vital for the rehabilitation centre but not only their centre, all the surrounding districts as well. These prisoners weren't hard core murders, they were people pushed beyond their limitations and cracked. The difference between life sentences and freedom for these guys was their lawyers. Helping these inmates and finding the right candidates meant vital screening and Eli could be just the lad for the initiation.

The chairman took his seat and waited patiently for his interviewee. Eli was escorted into the interrogation room and he recognised it. He felt uncomfortable.

"Relax son," commented the chairman as he saw the apprehension in the boy's eyes. "Yes, behind the glass are the other representatives who were with us yesterday, they are still watching and they are still assessing you. But this conversation is between you and me.

There is some more information I need to know and then I'd like to offer you something new. A very promising new proposition that has never been done before and as much as I do believe you are a very good contender; I still need proof.

You have a lot going for you Eli, you also have a lot going against you; so, let start. This proposal of yours is brilliant; however, your prior record demonstrates you did poorly at university. Did you deliberately fail?"

Eli shook his head, then realise he need to respond. "No, I just wasn't interested."

"Good that's good; so, with this proposal, you're are really interested in the outcome?" Eli nodded. "Excellent. You see that was another of my quandaries. If someone does something of this callibre for another and they fall out for some reason, then the deal often goes sideways, but if they are doing it for themselves, they have the nous to continue regardless of the relationship. I need to know do you want this for you too?"

Eli smiled and nodded. "Yes." The chairman saw the softness and light in his eyes. He felt confident he was reeling him in.

"You are also looking at Asian waters unlike your father."

Eli looked up in reproach, "What I need to know is, are you abandoning your fathers import business and starting your own or are you and your brother expanding?"

"We don't want anything to do with his business," Eli stated scoldingly. The chairman placed his hand to his ear to hear feedback from the adjoining room. Eli had forgotten they were there. He'd forgotten he was still being interviewed by a board.

"The physiologist says, you're your reactions are saying you're telling the truth." They both smiled. "You can relax now, we're all on the sameside." Eli gave more of a sighing grin as he felt much of the tension leave his body.

"Let me tell you what we would like to offer you." He paused from speaking as he revealed a folder. The chairman appeared to be most proud ofit. "It's the first of its kind around here and you are the test dummy if you like. Your success is vital to the ongoing success of the scheme and it could change the lives of thousands of good men caught up in shitty circumstances.

Unlike your university degree this is a Governmental University Apprenticeship Scheme. It goes for four years instead of three. It is completely over seen by several government departments. That's to protect you and the party who wants to employ you. Your books will be audited constantly through your apprenticeship but your company will be under government surveillance long after you complete your apprenticeship should you choose to continue your employment. This is to protect you and your brother."

As Eli scanned the files, he excitedly interrupted, "This is what I would tell dad, this is what I wanted, but he wouldn't listen, he always took short cuts." Eli was shaking his head in frustration.

"So, you do understand son?"

"Yeah," he was now excited as he sighed with relief as if finally, someone was listening to him. His gut always told him this sort of business option would work, it would be safe, it would be profitable, and you can get huge international government benefits, he knew all this, but his father and his family knew better ways, skanky ways, black market ways.

Eli kept mumbling as he was recalling all the discordances between he and his father. According to his father what Eli was learning at university was rubbish. He just needed his son to have a brilliant business degree so his father could teach him the real ropes of successful business like the rest of his family only Eli would be the boss because he had the degree. But now Eli could follow a dream that was bigger than him. He'd never done anything for himself before, this was new ground. This was exciting. He could feel the enthusiasm building inside of him.

"So, you're interested in the apprenticeship possibility? Its longer than your university degree but the outcome is far more beneficial for you and so many others who will follow in your footsteps."

Eli laughed to himself. "Balancing the scales," he mumbled under his breath. The mumble caught the chairman's attention "Gran," Eli paused a second, "You'd like her; she'd call this, balancing the scales."

"Karma," commented the chairman. He laughed as well. "I'll be honest I don't know if that works, but what I do know is from a practical perspective. These guys in here are dependent on us making this a huge success so they can have their lives back too. This small act could change the lives of thousands of men over time for the better, that's got to *account* for something. I'm not doing it for that. I'm pragmatic, I'm the money guy. If you become a success, we get more funds automatically to keep the success going without pleading, begging, or sacrificing. The people I answer to don't care what it is as long as it makes them look great." The chairman waited patiently for a positive reaction.

"We will give you all you need, do for you all that we can to make this work a success, but I'm not doing it for you. I'm doing it for my own reasons a well. What do you say?"

Eli took the file, nodded with a huge smile. The chairman stood up held out his hand and gave him a businessman's handshake.

"Welcome aboard son."

As Eli walked out of the room, he gave a wave to the board members behind the glass and with a cheeky grin said, "thank you."

He walked outside the door, he wanted to punch the air, jump up and down, but this was prison not civvy street, they'd probably lock him up for assault.

He would phone Liam that night with his exciting news. They were doing this. It was real. He could feel the wheels of success reeling through his body. He felt like a little boy again, all excited, dying to show Liam his new lizard.

The chairman left the interview room, had a brief interlude with the board members then returned to his private office. There was someone seated in the dark corner of the room. "Scotch," he asked, as he poured two glasses. "Well, we did it. We got them; both of them." He handed the glass to the visitor in the lounge.

"Good," responded the soft female voice. "Good." Gran breathed a sigh of relief as she raised her glass and sipped her scotch. She sat back contentedly in the chair and they continued their conversation.

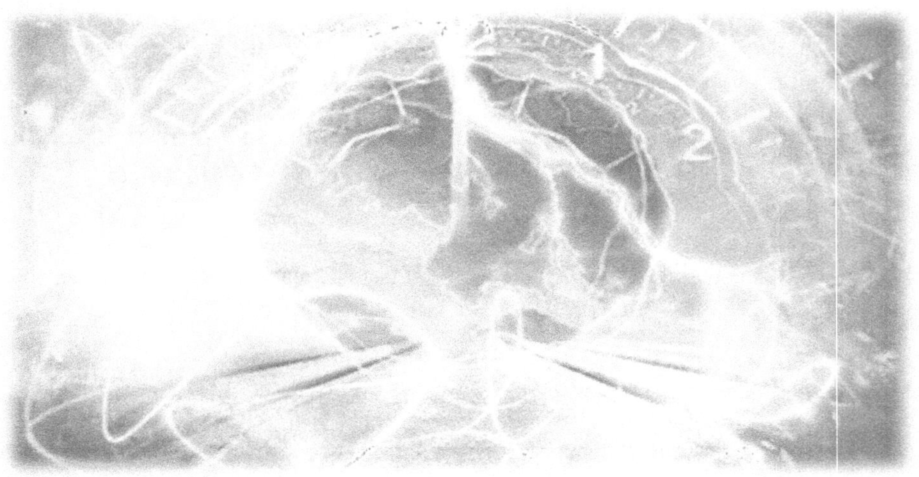

CHAPTER FOURTEEN

ONE GIANT STEP FOR MAN

The phone call that night although brief was impacted with excitement and enthusiasm from both boys. Liam was at first a bit dubious at all the government "big brother" concept but when Eli informed him of all the resourceful bonuses they would receive as well because they were so protected by governmental sources, he hoped his little brother knew what he was talking about.

Within a few weeks the bank finalized the sale of the business and all the deeds were delivered by his father's lawyer and placed in Liam's hands, with the optional proposal to maintain his services as his lawyer. According to the legal representative, with his knowledge and ability in reference to his fathers' business he would make an ideal candidate. He left his business card with Liam and asked him to call.

Liam graciously placed all the papers and his card on the coffee table and let the gentleman out. He returned to the lounge, collected the paperwork deliberately dumped the business card in the bin and proceeded to his father's office which would now officially be his.

Liam refused to see himself sitting in his father's shadow. Renovations were going to be necessary. He wanted someone young and innovative to redecorate. Someone with panache, style and technical know- how. Big move eliminating his past, he thought; even bigger move eliminating his father. Liam, in his late twenties had never really stepped out on his own before. Even though he was a loner, he always had the safety net of his family.

But this time, although he has Eli and Gran, he felt very much on his own. Flying without a net wasn't an uncomfortable feeling, but it certainly would be a new experience.

His path for the international chemistry research would allow him to travel several times a year at the same time do most of his work from home.

Same with the import business. He could travel to specific locations for trade and then he would work from home or a marketing warehouse. Internet was a marvelous business tool but with Elis's nous they should be able to create a remarkable market for their new products.

Alcohol, spirits, beer then we can diverse to some European markets for interesting international wines. There are some well-hidden markets in that area for the more sophisticated pallets. His father would buy cheap shit then he'd make a bucket. Liam and Eli would sell up market and supply top end grade booze for the more refined palate."

Eli explained that "with the taxes on booze the government will love us. We'll also need some advertising campaigns advertising our select product only. That way we have a hold on the retail market as well. Then you have the customer's wanting it. The retailer's wanting it. Merchandisers wanting it and they all come to us."

"You make it sound so easy?" remarked Liam

"Nah, if it was easy everyone would be doing it. This will take precision decision's, a carefully planned battleplan and a lot of patience. It won't fall into place; we have to create the places for it to fall into." Listening to Eli, Liam noticed that his young brother had the gift of the marketing gab. He could roll colloquialisms off his tongue as insightful captions.

Eli started scribbling on a piece a A4 paper. He was drawing diagrams and graphs with long term and short-term goals. Liam had never seen his brother show any sign of aptitude before. It was always the social parties, the booze, the fast cars, the irresponsible life style; this man before him had mathematical skills and intelligence. He was speaking trajectories and developments. He wanted to analyze strategies and tactics; this was language Liam had never seen stroke his brother's lips before.

Liam sat gob smacked; He had a business partner; a genuine honest to goodness business partner who knew what he was doing. He felt proud of him like a father to his son. Before his eyes his brother had blossomed into this clever business man.

Eli saw the bemused look on his face. "What?"

Liam didn't answer he simply smiled

"We don't have time for that." responded Eli "The paperwork for my apprenticeship is being drawn up as we speak. Both of us have to read it carefully. Really understand it. I have to find us a decent lawyer, then, sign it and get it witnessed." Eli paused and sighed, catching his breath, "Now do you want to keep the company name?"

"Do we need it?" questioned Liam hesitantly.

"Nah," stated Eli smiling confidently, "we're just two new kids on the block who are willing to create a great business with them." Then Eli remembered, "Dad or uncle created bad relations in this area don't know who, where or why. We need to get in fast, prove we can be trusted, prove we are worthy of their business and hope that's enough to save our asses I'm not saying "if," they find out who we are, I'm saying "when" and we need a good backup plan. Sales, service, demand, ongoing business without any monkey business with government support," he exhaled, "hopefully that will save our arses." The boys relaxed, drinking their coffee, then in the midst of their conversation, Eli stressed some demands.

Two things; one, get rid of that painting of the ship in dad's office, it was bugged. Two get rid of all his computer software and hardware equipment. The government had no proof to check his computers before but now it's different. We are to have nothing, NOTHING in that office that remotely connects you to his old company. His desk, his chair, his sofa, gone all of it. Get the walls checked for bugging devices, all that crap."

"My god the government must have been desperate." chided Liam in disgust.

"Government, not the government." Eli in exasperation exploded, "Your uncle." He paused then repeated his exasperating remark, "Our uncle." He grinned as he waited and watch for his brother's reaction and he got it. Complete unbelievable shock. Eli waited then he leant forward on the table.

"Promise me something Li, if you stop trusting me, if you stop believing in me, talk to me please. I don't know if they ever cared for each other or if they had a falling out, but their relationship was like the twilight zone.

Everyone thought they were the best of mates but they were both watching the other in case they got the knife in their back. Our uncle's house is bugged just as much a ours, mostly dad's office.

A lot of them would have been cleared out after dad's death. Our dear uncle's security team would have got rid of a lot of them because it was a police crime scene."

Eli continued explaining. "Remember the robbery about two months before dad's death. That's what gave me the idea of a robbery. That was our dear uncle. He was putting in new sound bugs. He always thought they weren't working. Apparently when anything went amok or awry dad always thought of his brother so he would investigate and many times found the incriminating evidence and instead of removing them, he would leave the room if he needed to talk in secret. This way he controlled everyone and all the information coming and going from the house." Eli started doing the twirling of the finger around the top of the head inferring someone was loopy. "Told ya, fucking fruitloops the lot of em." Waving his finger back and forth to Liam and him, "we're nuts, you and me, we're nuts, but we're the fricken sane ones, I'm tellin ya."

"It's like something out of Godfather," Liam mockingly laughed.

"It's like something out of 'Naked Gun; fuckin diabolical stupidity," responded Eli as they both broke out in ruckus hilarity at the utter disbelief at their fraudulent life. The portrayal of a perfect existence in a world of catastrophic mayhem. "Fuckin nuts, the lot of em but don't lose sight of any of them, they're all like loose cannons; freakin dangerous."

The boys continued establishing what they had in hand and what they needed to do. The contract day would be sometime in the next week, and that office needed to be sterilized. "We don't work for the government but for the next four years minimum we might as well be, so clean slate. I'd say they might try checking your computer as well only for components that involve the importing business. Without a warrant they cannot touch any of your other files unless there's a link, so clean it up too.

Eli took his big brother's hand in both of his, he held it tightly. Small tears welled in his eyes, "You always come back for me, you know that, you never ask why or whose fault it is, you just always come back for me. I'd have been lost without you this time. You've saved my life. Smultzy, I know, smultzy."

Liam laughed, "The old girl would-be impressed" he waited awhile, "I didn't realise it but you……. you, pretty much save mine too bro." He nodded as they both shared more intimate moments from their childhood before Liam had to leave.

Two days passed and the prison called Liam in to sign the apprenticeship contract to employ a prisoner for the period of four years while he completed his business studies in importing and exporting, advertising, governmental tariffs and laws and legals, and accounting.

Eli and Liam sat on the same side of the desk. This hadn't occurred for many years and both boys became aware of it and acknowledged it. The beginning of a fabulous partnership. As they sat with all the papers in hand, in walked a tall young slender Mediterranean woman. Eli stood up. He shook her hand and introduced his brother to their new international lawyer. She shook his hand, and seated beside him, placing her briefcase on the floor and her hands joined together on the desk as she sat up right waiting for the chairman and the government official to begin the proceedings.

The paper work was handed around and the lawyer received her copy. The boys watched as she perused every line carefully. She checked a couple of queries with the chairman for clarification then placing the paper in front of her on the desk, she attested she was satisfied. Then melodically she asked, "what have you boys decided to call your company?"

"I've been thinking about this," responded Eli, "I want something with both our names but something that won't be recognise on the international market. I was thinking Eliam Imports, if that's okay with you Liam?"

Liam excitedly interjected, "My thoughts were the same. I even came up with the same name only I added *international imports* after our name."

"Agreed," said Eli nodding his head. "Eliam International Imports it is then." Eli shook both of his brother's hands profusely with a huge smile on his face.

"Just write that on the top there please," instructed the lawyer to the chairman as she pointed to the second page of the contract. "Now I need you to sign here, here and here." She gave another contract to Eli "I need you declare your business name here, then sign here and here. And Liam I need you to do the same, write your business name, and sign here and here."

They all proceeded to follow the given instructions and after they did, she proceeded to take all contracts. She diligently witnessed, dated and stamped all of them. She then said, "all is done here, I'll have these delivered to the appropriate governmental departments this day and you should have your contracts legally bound within 14 days. She stood up, collected her bags, and held out her hand to again greet both of the boys, "Good luck gentlemen, we will be in touch very soon, a lot to discuss. However, we are restricted until contracts are legal. She handed both boys her business card. "Call me if you need any questions answered regarding your new enterprise, but after you get you contracts, please." She turned and shook the chairman's hand. "Been a pleasure as always Mr. Chairman I'll see my own way out thank you gentlemen." The door closed behind her.

The chairman stood up and held out his hand to Liam, I've heard a lot about you lad. You have to understand this project really means a lot to me and I'm so pleased both of you have decided to jump on board with us, as in the prison. You're both literally our test dummies. Your success could change the way rehabilitation works and how we can get really good men back into society.

"You consider me a really good man?" sniggered Eli.

"I consider all the men in here really good men, it's just no one ever told them that."

Eli giggled as he mumbled under his breath, "Gran would really like him," Liam also laughed.

"I'll take that as a compliment" responded the chairman as he began to depart the room. "You can have half an hour to discuss future plans then the guard will come to escort you out Liam. Eli, you can now find you own way back to your room or the computer room if you like. You will be monitored through hallway cameras but no longer under guard. However, should you require help there is always a button near the exit doors. A guard will respond."

Eli smiled in total surprise. The chairman continued. "You like that? Well, this is what I want for all the men, so don't fuck it up. Freedom is not where you live, it's who you are son. Freedom has to be inside of you. You can exist out there and still be imprisoned or you can live in here and be free, it's your choice. Being victim is a choice. I want all you guys to know true freedom and respect it; respect you."

Eli nodded as the chairman left believing he had the right man for the job. A feeling of almost freedom, is a hell of a lot better than incarceration. Eli didn't realise that his simple little choice to try to improve himself could change his entire existence. He nodded and agreed, "gotcha."

Eli turned to his brother, "sounds a lot like Gran don't you think?" He laughed, "She's haunting me," He threw up his arms and raised his voice, "the witch is haunting me," they both enjoyed the joke.

They had a lot to discuss and figure out. They had to legalize the business name. They had to start searching for more contacts, and an advertising slogan. All the little things that get overlooked, now was the time to construct them to secure the success of the project. It was slowly coming together, one step at a time.

Eli had programmed a five-year success plan which meant due to his studies, four years of that would be under the university tutorial and industrial help from the government. His brain was flashing with possibilities that were fathomless.

He thought about the chairman's words. 'Pretty cool, really, quite profound.' Eli never thought of himself as victim before. Now he saw he'd been living his entire life as victim. Always answering to other's needs. Is that why the chairman asked 'If I wanted this? It has to be for me. Is that why it feels so great? I'm doing for Liam but I'm really doing it for me, no…. I'm doing it *with* Liam; *with* Liam. The old bugger is right.   It doesn't matter where I am, I'm free as long as I'm free in me. "My choice," he scoffed.

So, this is what freedom feels like. He realised he was really smiling, and it felt good.

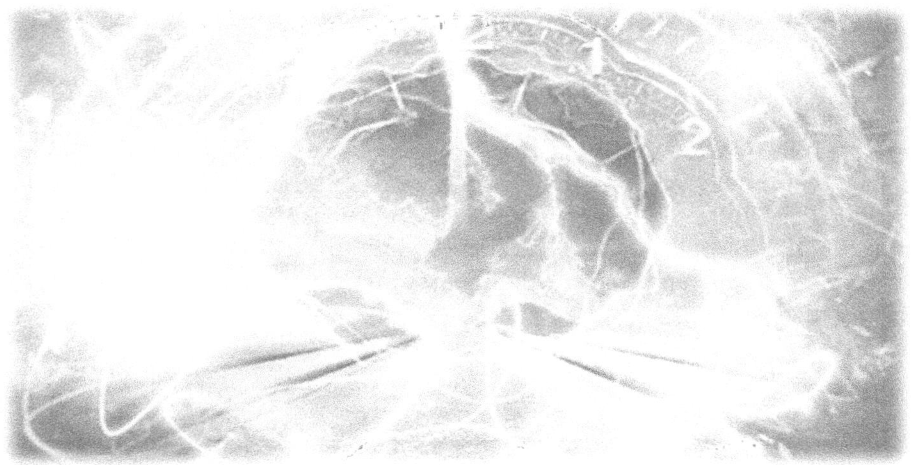

CHAPTER FIFTEEN

THINKING ON YOUR FEET

Learning to stand on your own two feet is a colossal feeling of independence but when everything starts happening at once it can knock the wind out of your sails.

Liam had to hand in a paper on his chemical research on the burning reactions of his suspected Lyme disease on his skin. Ever since he was born his skin and joints has been on fire. They diagnosed him very early in life with Lyme disease. His work along with many others researchers are striving endlessly to assist many young and old with this debilitating disease. He finds anything can set it off including stress so he has to be careful and aware.

Liam's body was starting to burn so he took his medication and walked into his father's office which was riddled with many a memory of a thrashing because he as a small child couldn't control the pain. An abusive merry go round. The more it hurt the more he would get abused, the more he got abused the more it would hurt. He smiled as he vindictively thought, 'it won't be a problem getting rid of you at all.' He turned his back and retreated from the room and the memories.

'Let's find someone with enthusiasm and pizzazz to crush you.'

Within an hour there was a response on his phone. A local company who states, "We knows the area." She likes to work with local builders and creators who also know the area. She would like to give him a quote. Would tomorrow be too soon. Liam swiftly answered and made the appointment for early the next day.

Next morning a fresh young vibrant woman walked into Liam'shouse believing the entire house needed renovations.

Liam directed her to the room. "This way; it's the office."

She walked into a huge dark room enclosed with book cases and long floor to ceiling heavy floral drapes. In the centre a huge heavy oak desk with matching furniture to encapsulate a room of intense power. She asked if the drapes could be pulled. Once the drapes were open the entire atmosphere of the room altered to an expansive light airy room exposing a huge back block of soft English gardens.

"Split personality," she commented.

"Sorry," questioned Liam.

"The room she has a dual personality." she explained. "How do you see the alterations taking place. What do you want to accomplish?

As he waved his hand over the vista he said "I want it all gone; all of it; the desk, chairs, book cases, books, the lot."

"Bad memories?" she quietly queried,

"The worst," he whispered.

"I'm sorry, but is this where your father was killed?" she questioned with empathy,

"No," he adamantly responded with hatred in his voice. "This is where he lived."

He turned and walked out the room with steadfast pace.

The assessor remained and started her quote. She had a few questions for the owner. Does he wish to sell the furniture, donate or destroy

When Liam returned, he apologized for his bad behaviour. The assessor asked her questions, and his response was he didn't care.

"You could donate it to a local charity and we can get an assessment on the price of all the pieces, then you can claim it on your tax and donate that to charity or use it to develop something that would have really pissed him off completely." She stared at him and grinned. "Hey if you're going to do the revenge thing, sometimes it pays to think like a woman."

Liam grinned as that was one of Grans sayings.

"Does that mean yes?" she questioned,

"Let's do it."

"Really?" she astounded reacted

He paused as he realised, he was beginning to like her. "I'd like you to check for bugs in the wall too please?"

"White ants?"

Liam pulled a face, and sarcastically said, "No"

"OMG. I'll get some communication people in here immediately,"

Liam smiled as he watched her expression of shock. "Get rid of that picture on the wall as well." Referring to the massive wall portrait of the Aragon 23 sail ship.

The assessor asked jokingly, "Is it bugged too? Liam smiled indicting yes "oh, oh, oh, oh," she responded as if she didn't know how to respond.

Liam laughed, "I'll leave you with it." he left the room happier than he was before. Her shockwave at the preposterousness of the lifestyle that existed here, concurred with his.

After an hour she sent a message to his phone, expressing she had a free quote for the removal of furniture as he was donating to a charity. Communications will be there tomorrow if he wants them. Carpet and drapes, removal to charity, but if he agrees she needs to say yes to all these contractors now so they can turn up the next day if that is suitable. She has to arrange a time tables otherwise there will be trucks everywhere and that is very unprofessional.

She waited impatiently for his response pacing up and down but he quietly turned up at the door. He was smiling at her.

"Arrange your time table." He smiled, "Will you be here?"

'Yes, someone has to keep this rabble running on time." she timidly replied.

"Well then maybe afterwards I could take you out for a hard-earned dinner. You'll have deserve it. By that time, I may have a better idea of how to redress this room."

She calmly responded, "I don't usually mix business with pleasure but this time I might make an exception. I'd like that."

"Me too. Do what you need to do and I'll see you tomorrow." Liam left the room.

He couldn't stop smiling. He hadn't been out with anyone since long before his father died. He hadn't given it much thought. Now his life seems to want to get back to some sort of new normal all at once. He hadn't felt this happy for years, even before his father died; even with Gran. This last week everything was changing. He was as if all the shackles were being removed.

For the first time in his entire life, he wasn't victim anymore. He never knew how that felt before. This was all new to him. It was liberating, exciting, unexplored territory, he wanted to keep riding high on this wave.

He realised he has never seen any of his father's family happy. They are all in business, they are married or in relationships, but he'd never seen any of them smile simply because they were alive. He'd never seen any of them say they love their business or their family. There were relationships and they were falling in and out of love, but none of them were…. He paused to himself as he tried to find the appropriate word.

None of them were free. The decisions they chose were made from the circumstances, the lifestyles they were bound to. They all sold their souls for money. He concluded 'no wonder I never knew freedom, they don't know what it is. None of them could ever show me how to get it. They ran away, all around the world and they are all still imprisoned.

Except for Gran maybe. Every word that comes out of that woman's mouth is a lesson of inspiration of some kind. She doesn't speak for the sake of speaking; every word, every sentence has a function. She doesn't just talk it, she lives it, and none of them see that. "She can see it; they can't," he whispered to himself.

He went to his office and completed his thesis and prepared it to be emailed to his new consortium in Europe. He was proud of his publishing's and this new variance should advance much of his new research even further.

The night had taken its toll and he packed it in ready for a new day of noise and commotion. He would start processing new ideas for his office and the computerised set up he required for his new business in the morning. Eli gave him a quick rundown and the boys always had the best of equipment from their father's business. 'It would have all been tax deductible,' thought Liam. 'It wasn't as if he gave it to us because he cared, but we thought he did and that was all that mattered. As gran says, it's not who he was that counts, it was how we reacted to him that mattered."

The morning started early with the sound of the arrival of a huge removal truck. The front door bell pealed through the second floor as Liam made his way down stairs from his office. He opened the door to two huge removalists with documents requesting the removal of 8 pieces of large furniture from an office plus 20 smaller pieces.

"Happy with that, sign here, and we'll start." explained the taller of the two gents. Liam signed the paper work and ushered them to the office.

They placed plastic shields on their shoes, and proceeded to follow him. The two burley men stood in the corner of the room discussing the best plan of attack. They walked around the room testing the furniture to see which can be unassembled or which pieces are all one. Liam stood at the door watching and listening.

He understood very early in the piece these men knew exactly what they were doing and did not need any assistance at all. The second of the gentlemen caught Liam's eye, "you want all of this gone, right?"

Liam stepped up, "Yes." The men looked at each other, nodded and without saying a word knew exactly what they were going to do.

They proceeded to the truck and unlocked the backdoors. The threw out piles of underlays to protect the furniture. They emptied their truck preparing it for loading. Swiftly they returned with all the equipment they would need to move the heavy-laden furniture from the office. Liam decided he would be in the way and was about to vanish upstairs when a soft friendly voice of the assessor echoed through the front door.

"I see they have started. Is everything okay?"

Liam smiled, "is now."

"Oh, was there a problem?" she looked at him and caught his smile. She then coyly realised he was referring to her. "Have you any plans about how you wish to redecorate?" She tried to maintain a professional attitude however she had dropped her guard the day before and now she had to re-establish some form of equilibrium.

Liam ushered her upstairs to his office. She felt uncomfortable being upstairs, but when she arrived, she saw it was a floor of offices, like a multiple doctor's offices. She was expecting bedrooms or comfortable rooms for families, but it was cold establishment. She thought "what a waste of beautiful space."

Liam went to his filing cabinet and pulled out different plans he'd been creating, but none really satisfied him. He explained he needed several monitors and screens, computers but that meant cords everywhere.

"Bluetooth, WIFI," she smirked feeling very cocky.

Liam found himself spellbound for she also understood the intricacy of computerization setups. She stepped up to the designs "Do you mind." Liam stepped back as he felt himself melt into the waft of her perfume. She started asking about the dimensions and suggested better ways to use the space in the room, creating light in the right area without glare on his screens. Liam found himself total enthralled with everything she was saying. She was smart, creative, intelligent, and beautiful.

The more she spoke the more Liam was seduced. Expecting a shock reaction, Liam explained cautiously how he may need a hidden computer somewhere so he can converse with his brother in prison.

She responded with professional discipline. That's software. If the prison has specific software or links, they will give it to you to access. If you hide anything you automatically look guilty. I don't know your situation but if it has to do with your brother and the prison, the appearance of total honesty needs to be the ambiance. I don't care how crooked you become as long as the ambiance declares you to appear innocent.

Liam looked at her in shock.

She continued, "Your business is your business. Mine is to make it look perfect."

He was impressed by her up fronted ness. 'It's honest, trust me." He lowered his head and grinned.

"Still, none of my business." She interjected quickly, re-gaining her professional stance.

She took out her notebook computer and started opening up different designer company apps that were local who could give him unique and extremely functional designs, from old fashioned antique wood to computerised sci fi

She laughed as she stated, "sci fi holograms are not quite the choice yet, but don't disregard it in future specifics. That's where this group come in handy. Creative innovative and futuristic, maybe a little too advanced for some but from what I can see by the rooms upstairs, you and your brother were also technically advanced. You may enjoy some of their products. I can arrange a video interview.

This is another, not quite so computer orientated but they have potential for future advancement if you wish to design your own.

"I need to run this stuff by Eli," stated Liam feeling a little overwhelmed at the enormous possibilities,

"If I may interfere again and you can tell me to mind my own business, but Eli, your brother I presume," she paused for waiting for him to concur, "will be using the best equipment the prison has to offer. This is your equipment; this is what you will be comfortable to work with. You are looking at long term plans. We'll mention that to the designers and let them work with you with the option to alter if unsatisfactory."

Her advice was expletory; all of a sudden everything became clear. "You're right of course." He too decided to sound more professional. "Get me interviews with three computer tech orientated designers. No wood, clean like a scientific lab. Futuristic is good, sci fi definitely, set up to be easily managed. I'll leave that with you." He stood up and smiled, "Are we still on for tonight"

"Most definitely, more than ever, we should finish here about 6.30. Is that okay?"

He smiled, "Perfect," as he started walking out, "Now I'll have to find a new topic of conversation, but,"

"Décor is not all I do. I'll have you know I'm a very interesting person thank you," came her humorous rebuttal.

Standing in a humorous defensive pose Liam replied, "I look forward to finding out." He giggled and left the room to go work in another office.

A call from downstairs echoed the completion of the first truck. "Denver's on his way now for the carpet and drapes."

Standing at the door of a very empty room, the assessor could see huge possibilities, for without the furniture the space appeared even larger. There was a knock at the open door, "Communications; I believe we have some bugs to destroy?"

"Oh, please this way." She ushered them all into the room, completely unaware of all the equipment needed to quote 'destroy some bugs' "How long will you be?"

The technician opened up his laptop which was linked to a van outside and began immediately scanning the room, "you can see where a lot have been. Messy jobs, very unprofessional, should have got us. They've been ripped out, so they are inactive. Do you want them cleaned up? Take twenty maybe twenty-five minutes."

"Yes please, then leave you invoice with me and I'll have you paid within 7 days." Brilliant, she responded to herself. For a brief moment she had forgotten the reputation of this house, and the secrets it held.

The time flew by rapidly and the work was finished, assessed and the van was on its way when Denver's larger than life carpet and curtain van arrived. Out stepped two very fit young men who needed to know where they were to work.

They were ushered to the vacant office and saw the articles that needed removing. They would need tall ladders, and tools to remove the drapes and accessories, then uplift the recently renewed carpet. Before they proceeded, they made sure no one else would be entering the room. They were assured that would be the case so the interior furnishings staff started dry steaming the carpet and curtains.

This seemed an unusual practice and when the assessor asked why, they responded, "this is all brand new, hardly touched, exceptional seconds. We super bond this, it's as good a new. We can re-lay this without any delay."

Their response was a surprise as well. At dinner that night that was one of the queries the assessor asked. Liam relaxed back in the restaurant seat completely unprepared for the inquisition.

"Have you ever renovated a house after a death?" Liam scanned her eyes as she shook her head. He recalled, "You can smell the death all through it." he deliberated a little longer. "My father wasn't in the house very long after his death, but I could still smell the stench of his blood and foul odour of his death so, I re-carpeted and furbished all the rooms down stairs. The whole echelon may have been psychosomatic but I couldn't enter the house without feeling the stench of his dead body cricking through every part of me."

"I'm sorry for prying I didn't realise. It's just the boys steamed it and told me it was new I didn't understand why you wanted it ripped up if it was new, that's all."

He leant in and placed both elbows on the table, and began to speak flirtatiously "I'm glad," he paused a minute with a childish grin on his face, "I want you to know that when I like someone I fall in completely and I really like you. I really want to spend more time with you, I want you to know me, not that there's much to know, I want to be with you and ridiculous as it seems I see myself wanting to spend the rest of my life with you."

Feeling very romantic, Liam found he couldn't take his eyes off her nor could he take the smile off his face. "I know we've only just met and this is going way too fast, but this is me. I live in a very cocooned world. I had no idea what my father was up to or his business, but my brother did." He paused a minute and judged what he just said. He sat back almost ashamed of what he was thinking. "No, that's not quite true. I knew my father, and I didn't like him. So, I studied chemistry so I wouldn't have anything to do with him, so I wouldn't have to communicate with him or be with him. It was my form of rebellion, escapism if you like. I just didn't realise……" he kept thinking. He gave a sigh "my poor Eli he got the straddled with the lot. He says I saved him but I abandoned him. I abandoned him to that lot."

He began to remove himself from the table. "Sorry you don't need to hear this."

She reached for his hand, "If you want me to be here forever there are some things I may need to know and some I don't, but are you now going to abandon me too, the minute you let me get close? Is that what you do also?"

He stared at her in astonishment, wondering why anyone would want to be involved with someone with so much baggage.

"We all have baggage, some good some bad." She took his hand in both of hers. 'It's just a matter of how pretty you tie the bow," she whispered.

He laughed as he reciprocated and took her hands in both of his. "Wow you are like my Gran."

She responded with a look of disapproval "Really?"

Liam relaxed and started to open up more, "Our world as kids was a world of anger, pain, abuse and violence sometimes, but in the centre of it was this harbinger of peace with inspirational quotes of words and colloquiums that helped me see it all through. Even dad's murder, she sees the concept, that it is an unpaid debt, and in the past Eli was the victim of sorts. She cannot hate or judge Eli for fulfilling some past commitment. She helped me see it that way so I can still love him and not judge him and then walk the same continuous path of pain later. You don't remind me of my Gran," he emphasized, "just the beautiful person inside."

She smiled and mouthed the word "thank you." He mimicked "you're welcome."

"Now I have to tell you something," she quietly responded. "I can't marry you or anyone, that would be unfair." Liam was taken back, "I have idiopathic fibrosis I don't have long to live. And to marry someone knowing the pain this would cause them is extremely selfish. But I will stay friends with you if you like and we can have a loving relationship however I've thought about this for years and,"

"Well, that means we have to move quickly." he gushed with a huge smile on his face. "We need to get this underway immediately so I can spend as much time with you that is allowed. I won't ask how long; I'll simply spend every moment making you as happy as possible in the time you have."

"You don't understand that's not my purpose." she explained

"No, it's mine," he smiled and gazed into her eyes, "you know you have very pretty eyes. Will you marry me as soon as possible so I can look into those beautiful eyes for as long as possible."

She giggled with embarrassment, "Why, are you pregnant." He laughed with her.

"Don't run away, I'm a professional at that, I know all the lurks and quirks. I'm a very rich man I can make you happy. I will give you every wish you could ever ponder. I will spoil you rotten."

"And they'll all think I married you for your money," she laughingly shook her head.

"Well, they'll be wrong. You are feeling sorry for me because I'm pregnant," he gaffed.

"Now you're just being foolish. This has got to be the most ridiculous and outlandish idea you've ever had," she responded shaking her head

"It's a winner," Liam threw his arms up in the air and the entire restaurant turned and looked

"Are you crazy?" she questioned.

Liam quietened down. "There's a story about some really clever guy who would always create these crazy ideas and if no one liked them he would do them because they were determined to be a success."

"Walt Disney," she responded,

Liam queried "You know the story?"

"He would run suggestions by his board and if they rejected it, he knew it would always be a success. Yes, everyone knows it." she answered.

"If your disease puts you on a time limit, we may have time, we may not but sitting here quibbling over it is wasting it. Let me share a few years of happiness, real happiness with you. I can't say I love you for I don't know what that truly is I only know my perception of it. But I will give you all that I have no strings attached, that's everything I have including me." He waited for some response.

She had to admit, "I haven't smiled this much in my entire life, since I met you." She nodded in agreement, "I think I would like that, yes."

Liam moved around closer to her "you lose," he whispered, "you're stuck with me," and he bent over to taste her lips. "If I ever forget to kiss you at least once a day or hold you or tell you I love you, remind me, please remind me. I know that sounds smultzy."

"I kinda like smultzy at the moment," she responded.

"Eli will be impressed." His fiancée queried why. "He always wanted a baby brother." They both burst out laughing as their final course arrived.

"Especially when you inform him who the mother is," their laughter filled the room. They both embarrassingly apologized to the other guests as they continued wining and dining late into the night.

When they left the restaurant after dinner, they ambled arm in arm up the street, embracing each other laughing and giggling like young teenagers. Liam queried whether she wanted to return to his house or did she want him to return to hers.

In her tipsy state she gave him her opinion of his cold estate and declared although she had no idea what the sleeping accommodation looked like but she would prefer the warmth of her apartment.

Liam defensively informed her there were several luxuriantly attired bedrooms in the house and he'd be surprised if she didn't find one of them suitable to her sophisticated taste. However, after much ado they both decided to retire at her unit.

The next day Liam proudly exhibited five of his spacious uniquely furnished main and master bedrooms plus two extreme plush and comfortable guest bedrooms. Reacting with a very cocky supercilious smirk on his face, he remarked, "They are all yours. Take your pick."

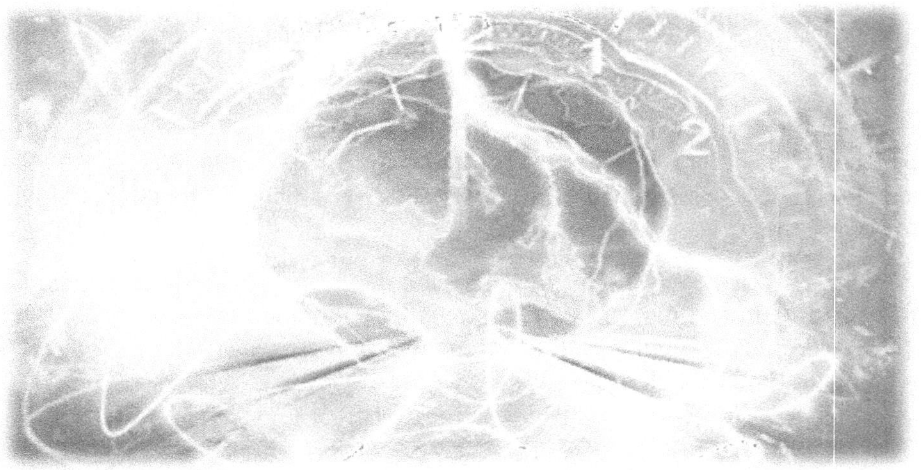

CHAPTER SIXTEEN

TRANSFORMATIONS

"Are you fucking crazy?" chuckled Eli as he received the news of his brother's upcoming nuptials at their next cordial visit. "Man, when you do crazy, you really do crazy." He laughed, then he turned to the guard who escorted Liam in. Putting his arms out in spread eagle "Permissions to hug my brother, he just got engaged?"

"We don't do that to you anymore." responded the guard sarcastically. "You fuck up, you're dead." Liam and Eli stared at him insurprise. "You don't know do you?" stated the guard in surprise. "Word of what you're doing here has spread like a virus. There are over three hundred guys out there as well as other rehabilitation centres who want to sign up to do your program. You fuck up they'll kill ya; their families will kill ya." He smirked as he delivered his information.

Eli pulled a face as he mumbled, "no pressure." The two men echoed his response. There was silence then Eli exploded "I can hug you." the guard echoed "we all can…. give you a hug that is," then a loud call bounded from three of them, "group hug." The guard politely wished him good luck as he laughed and left the room.

Eli was completely flummoxed by his brother's new news but he finally came to the solution, "you're a big boy now, go be happy," Liam felt happy and his disposition exposed it. Eli had to finally comment, "she's done something to you. You haven't stopped smiling since you came in here." He threw his hands in the air "I have never seen you this happy in your entire fucking life man. I don't know whether to be happy for you or have you tested for barbiturates."

Liam put his arm around his brother's shoulder. "I want you to be my best man." Eli stepped back stunned at the suggestion. Smiling and proud, he wanted to accept immediately, but doubted the possibility.

Shaking his head, he retorted, 'Maybe they'll allow the wedding but not a reception. I'll check it out but." he paused, picked his brother up and spun him around, "My brother's getting married, wow."

They eventually sat beside each other at the table, both silent but aware of the enjoyment of sharing their closeness again.

"Have the contracts come through yet," Eli queried. Liam shook his head indicting no, however, he was anxious to inform him of the new transformations that have taken place in the old office of their fathers. For the next couple of hours, as Eli took notes, the conversation was about all the new renovations taking place in the big room and how the introduction of new equipment all needed to be in synchronised with the equipment Eli would be using in the prison system.

Eli informed Liam of the progress being made around his dwelling as well, because some substantial funding had been approved for university training projects a new area of the prison was being set aside for those who wish to participate, so he will be one of the first candidates' testing all this new equipment. This was new ground for all contenders then they both echoed, "no pressure."

Liam was concerned about his office upstairs. It was completely independent. It is his chemistry research. It has international programs connected to Europe. Eli caught on. He was gloating for a moment. Downstairs is the pacific and upstairs is Europe. His clever research brother was patting himself on the back for he had an international business in his house.

The reason Liam was fanning his peacock feathers was because he was an extreme recluse. He hid in his research lab for years. He spoke to no one, socialised with no one. Now look at him. He was a new man. Eli patted him on the back, "I'm proud of you man, but I always was. But hey this new man, wow, where have you been hiding him. He's alive and movin' man."

Suddenly Eli stood up and spun on his feet pointing to Liam started humorously taunting him "You've had sex. My god you've been laid." He was laughing, teasing and taunting and carrying on like a banshee. Liam started feeling defensive but Eli was on his humorous roll. "Wow she must be good. What did she do with my brother?"

Liam sat quietly embarrassed. "Having fun?"

"Fuck yeah, I haven't laughed this much in years. And never because, MY BROTHER GOT LAID. Did you tell her you were a virgin?

"I am not a virgin," he splattered

"Well, you're not now and wanking doesn't count," he joshed.

"Finished?" demanded Liam hoping that Eli's humour at his expense had reached its climax.

Eli then finalised his smart alec remarks, "she's pregnant?"

"No, I am," rebutted Liam's proud of his comical response.

Eli slammed his hand on the table, and laughed out loud "I knew it,"

"Thought you'd want a baby brother" Liam's snidely remarked.

"Nah…. but can I have a horse," Eli chucked so hard he nearly fell over. Liam reached out ready to grab him. Liam hadn't seen Eli so stupidly happy and humorous for years either. This was how he remembered him. Eli's wicked sense of humour, with his ongoing taunting and endless teasing, as if on happy gas. Once he started, it was hard to stop.

Then the realisation that they were both experiencing fun bought them both back to earth. "300 guys, do you believe him?" frowned Eli.

Liam shrugged his shoulders, "but if we can give them this after their lives of shit,"

"And there he is, my droll brother," responded Eli. They both sat in silence for a minute as if all the excitement exhausted them. They started making arrangements for the week for a lot of new information will be arriving along with the setting up of all the new equipment. The truth was they had exhausted their conversations and for the first time in their reconciliation, there was an awkward silence as they both decided to depart. Liam pressed the button to be escorted out. "Call will ya?" he echoed back to his brother.

Liam's fiancé was now staying with him, she hadn't moved in yet but she spent most of her available time with him. Her decision to become Liam's wife hasten up the renovations to his office rapidly. It was starting to adapt a very sci-fi presence to new business and Liam was very impressed with the upgraded equipment. As the new and latest technology adorned what used to be a very stoic room Liam's enthusiasm to re-enter the room altered. The new technological laboratory was fresh and innovative and it created an ambience of futuristic business advancement with opportunities to excel.

Tradesmen and technical engineers were still present as Liam had to answer the front door. There standing before him was the chairman and his offsider. "You are expecting us? he queried as Liam displayed shock at his appearance.

"The contract was due today, we have it," stated the chairman as he waved his bureaucratic portfolio in front of Liam.

Liam stammered as he gestured for them to enter the foyer. "I assumed it was going to be posted,"

The chairman and a slender young red-head entered the lobby with all their gear, "This is my assistant Gyps and she will help you set up your equipment with both the government facility and the prison. She's actually the only one I trust." He paused as he started looking for an entrance to an office. Upon realisation Liam ushered them to his newly designed workplace.

"Now this *is* impressive. Who's responsible for this?"

A small female voice echoed from behind him, "I am,"

Liam rushed over and escorted his fiancé over to the chairman and Gyps and he introduced her.

She professionally countered "I have a company that deals with all forms of renovations, and computerisation is one of our highest formats." She handed the chairman a business card with all her details. "If you require alternate equipment or something extra, this is the number to call." Liam stood proudly beside her with his arm around her waist as she promoted the reason for her existence.

The chairman asked Gyps, "Can you work with this."

Gyps quietly and professionally answered, "Yes sir," Meanwhile her mind is screaming "CAN I. Let me at it."

The chairman then turned to Liam, "You need to verify some paper work then I'll be on my way." He handed Liam the briefings, "If it's okay with you and Eli of course I'd like to allow Gyps to scan your books and paper work at least once a week as per Eli's projects, reasons being as this is the experimental model, we want to nip all glitches in the bud early.

We have had a huge response from many other contenders and although that sounds very promising, not all are appropriate contenders. We as in I would like to make sure there are no weak links for future misappropriation and some of them will want it for that purpose, so if we have high maintenance fire walls to nip them in the bud early, we won't lose the innocent to the guilty and in this business, I can have a thousand brilliant contenders and one defunct, and the defunct gets all the attention and the entire program will get axed due to some biased goody two shoes.

That's why I have Gyps. She's the best. She can pick off a flee at a hundred metres. You need her on your team." Liam scanned the paper work and all was as it should be, so the chairman signed it off and returned it back to him in a huge documented folder. The Chairman re-scanned the room again and exited with a very impressed nod of approval.

"And as for your young lady", referring to Liam's fiancé, we'll be doing some business as well, not as elaborate as this, but definitely updating. I'll show my own way out," he shook Liam's hand and departed.

Liam stood for a few minutes and thought 'another whirlwind. Nothing happens quietly anymore. He wondered, was this to be the pace of his new life? This constant ability to think incessantly on your feet. The ability to make decisions while walking. That was his father's life and he never had time for anyone. Liam embraced his fiancé again then kissed her on the forehead.

Referring to his father Liam mumbled, "He didn't have you," He kissed her tenderly again and reassured himself, 'as long as I have you, whirlwind or not, everything will be a breeze.'

Gyps felt embarrassed interrupting them but she needed to start and required more information from Liam. His fiancé parted explaining how she had to go work for a living. Liam briskly returned to Gyps and gestured for them both to get started. As she worked through her programs and data, she then synchronised them on all the different computerised equipment. She would then disappear for ten minutes to talk to the communication representatives then return. Liam assumed she was upgrading his equipment and he wanted to know what she was doing.

She laughed with him, "Oh no, I'm not upgrading yours. I'm getting upgrades on mine. By syncopating ours I can talk to you securely and vice versa. Your equipment is top grade, and so is mine but to stay in sync with you securely I will need some new software, and that will keep the programs matching securely for several more years maybe? Your computerware hardware and software was not on the agenda, but it is perfect for ensuring the success of the program. Many businesses do not have the latest in equipment and their software leaves a lot to be desired. What you have done is created a criterion we need to work with for total success."

Liam flustered that he didn't install his lab to make business difficult for others.

"Oh, don't worry; it won't; but it gives us an excellent platform to initiate the success of the program from."

Liam realised he felt uneasy but he didn't recognise he was in victim mode. Gyps noticed the stress in his eyes, "I'm also an interim prison psychologist. Relax leave the worrying to me. You just be successful, that's what you do best. I'll take care of the rest. That's what I do best." She smiled as she continued to install all the apps and programs; she needed to have all systems comply.

"Do you mind if I return tomorrow? I'll go to the prison now and set the diagnostics up and hopefully all the dominoes will fall into place tomorrow and you can both commence.

Also, with your permission I will return once or twice a month to oversee everything, not your business you understand, only the things the government will audit in reference to this apprentice program."

Liam was hesitant.

Gyps again recognised he needed reassurance, "It's not your business they will be auditing it is the…. Oh, let me think... hacking. Illegal stealing of accounts etc.

You're not the only one who can get access to this program once it is installed. You will be working with the pacific. Now I'd like to say they are really nice people but as the chairman said, one defunct and you lose millions. They would not be after your business they would want government access. Now they cannot get it but it doesn't mean they won't try. These aren't business men. These are really clever kids. So, it isn't for your protection as much as it is mainly ours."

She shook his hand then quietly departed.

'Another whirlwind.' sighed Liam

All of a sudden, after weeks of utter chaos and commotion, it was quiet. His fiancé was at work; the communication installers were gone; Gyps and the chairman were gone; silence. He stood in the middle of the foyer and looked around him and he had nothing to do, nothing to fix up, prepare, remedy or rectify, everything was done; no whirlwind.

A point of realisation struck him. Silence is great if you want to read about other people's lives. Silence is great if you want to watch the world go by. Silence is great if you don't want to participate; but, the whirlwind, now that's an experience.

Even though it's fast, you are participating, experiencing, creating and thinking on your feet, and as long as the whirlwind doesn't absorb your soul to emptiness and you make the things you love a part of that whirlwind, it won't control you. You are still free to control it. Now I know why Eli loved the fast life. I judged it as empty, unfulfilling. It wasn't the fast life; it simply was life. Now he realised he would be living his life the same way. The very things he condemned for so long.

Liam's fiancé returned very excited "I have wonderful news. A friend who has a restaurant wants to do our wedding. She says they can arrange a celebrant in the restaurant under an arch while the guests sit at the reception tables watching. I know it's unusual, but the archway is in the garden and I was hoping that this way Eli could make a best man speech as we are not having church. I mean if I am going to go to hell it will be for worst things than this. What do you say? At least think about it?"

She held both his hands in hers near her breast and her pleading eyes melted Liam's heart, "Victimisation will be one of them," he laughed as he held her. "Yes," he whispered out loud, "I'd like Eli to give a speech, but I don't know how the system works. I like your idea. Tell your friend yes if that is really what you want. The answer is yes."

She embraced his neck and kissed him over and over again like a little child. She started for the door and returned again to kiss him but this timeLiam grabbed her hand. He pulled her close to him and kissed her long and deep. "That's so unfair," she uttered, but then he ushered her out the door. "Whirlwinds, gotta love em," he smirked.

The next day when Gyps arrived with the chairman, they had to evaluate the software, then as they were about to depart Liam approached the chairman about his upcoming nuptials and how he wanted Eli to be a part of the celebration.

Liam unassuredly explained how he understood that Eli was a murderer and that would make this decision difficult, but if it was possible for just one afternoon could his brother attend his wedding. The chairman turned glared at him in stunned amazement. They both stood in silence for a minute and Liam saw the strange look on his face.

"I have never looked at Eli as a murderer. I don't see any of those men as murderers. I've seen murderers and they are heartless, soulless, hell in their eyes demons who have lost their souls. He doesn't have the heart to kill unless he has been seriously provoked and I'm going to say he was incessantly provoked. The problem with the system is your father cannot be tried for the crime. Eli was tried for his unacceptable reactions to your father's behaviour. Do you see him as a murderer?"

Liam flustered as he realised what he had said. "It' not you it's the system," Liam responded.

"Fuck the system," responded the chairman. "It's your opinion that counts."

As Gyps walked out passed both of them, she mentioned. "His watch guard, the one who attends to Liam, would be an ideal plus one," she commented to the chairman as she straddled beside him. "He has been with Eli and Liam from the beginning. At least he knows both of them." She walked on a head of the chairman as he turned to Liam,

"Yes, we'll arrange a guard to be his plus one if that's okay and let us know when the event is happening and we'll organise some time. He's not allowed alcohol or drugs and you will have to have the suit measured at the prison. Keep in touch son." With those words he left the house through the front door.

Liam did keep in touch. He was quite jubilant about having a wedding with his brother as his best man. Liam refrained from inviting old family members for he was convinced they would focus their facetious bias for his father on his ceremony. Liam stood his ground, he refused to have anyone, for any reason, destroy the most wonderful day of his life because they wanted retribution. It had been almost four years now and his father's family still had not altered their severe opinions of a cold-hearted gold-digging son.

Gran was the exception but she always was. He was excited to introduce her to his lovely future bride and he wasn't reticent in any way. He was displaying pleasure and exhilaration, a personality that had been hidden for a lifetime.

Gran expressed to his fiancé "my goodness deary you have him bewitched. Who is this young man?" They all spent the afternoon together and the young fiancé did everything she could to impress her future Gran. Gran took the young lass's hand, "Calm down my child. He loves you like no other. You have his heart, soul and mind. His world is small and you are all he sees. You can do no more. If you can love him in the same way, you will have given him more than I could ever ask for." She gave her a hug and then they parted.

Later Liam came and sat beside his Gran, "You approve?"

"Like you need my approval" she responded curtly.

He laughed and shook his head, "Nah"

"But such a smile I have never seen since you were young at the resort with your mother. You and Eli laughed your lungs out that year, I'm so glad you had that chance to share it. Everything went watermelon shaped after that. Now you have some joy back. My Liam is happy again. Enjoy your time with her."

Gran felt a coldness within the soul of Liam's new love. This young lass tried too hard to impress. She was happy and jovial on the outside, but lacked inner heart. She knew she shouldn't judge but something was amiss and she couldn't quiet put her finger on it.

Liam looked at his Gran, curious to know if she knew the truth, but Gran avoided his gaze indicating it didn't matter what she knew and not to ask.

She patted his hand and encouraged him to go join his love. He obeyed graciously.

All was set in place. All arrangements were made. Liam paid for the restaurant for everyone and the flowers and the celebrant. The room was decorated with scented candles and orchids. A two-tier wedding cake was decorated in white with a touch of yellow to compliment the orchids. The simplicity of the celebration and the dignity of the room impressed Liam. This expressed his future wife's grace, her debonaire style, her class, her elegance.

Everything about her made him smile all the time. Eli arrived with his guard both dressed elegantly in silver grey suits to match the groom. As a gift from Liam, he allowed the guard to have whatever suit he wanted as well and the guard chose the same as the Eli, so Liam asked if he would like to be his groomsman. The guard was honoured. Liam thought, Gyps was right, the guard was ideal.

The bride and groom stood before the celebrant and swapped their vows as Liam was mesmerized by his Mediterranean princess. Eli gave a humorous and honourable speech on how proud he is to have Liam as his brother and how over whelmed he is to have her as his sister and he welcomed this gracious woman to their very non-gracious world.

Liam danced with his wife then Eli danced with his new sister. The bride and groom departed after the cake was cut and so did Eli with his guard.

The bridal couple headed to the Caribbean for their honeymoon then back to business for both of them. Meanwhile Eli started studying. He had to do the introductory courses; the courses that introduced him to all the basics rules and regulations that this apprenticeship required. This part of the course would take two weeks then the boys would officially have to start their business apprenticeship.

The whirl wind was steadying and Liam was content that he remained standing.

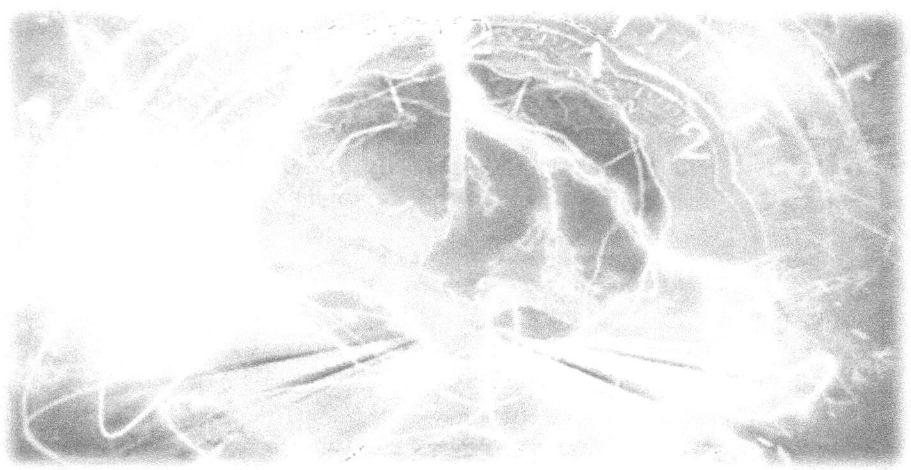

CHAPTER SEVENTEEN

BUSINESS AS UNUSUAL

The happily married couple sailed, swam and tanned. They loved and wallowed in each other's company every minute of the days. The two weeks passed too quickly for both of them. They returned to their home where new alterations were being prepared to start to the upstairs rooms. It would be designed for comfort to accommodate Liam's lab along with his European computer office but downstairs was his hub of industry.

Liam's wife continued her business as usual and worked and Liam began both of his new prominent positions. One as President of his importing business and the other as a mere chemist researcher for the European company.

In the initial year Eli was at the helm of the importing business, while Liam was the face. It was a year of firsts for Liam. Eli had experienced this phenomenon before but this experience was entirely new territory for Liam. Due to his inexperience, he was expecting drama and catastrophic errors, but they didn't arise. Eli covered all areas of development with backup plans allowing elaboration for his older brother as well. As Liam became more confident, he found himself stepping up more and as he advanced, the company started expanding and growing stronger as well.

Eli produced and promoted a package online with business strategies that proved to be innovative and productive. He found an exciting niche market then expanded to a more open market allowing the niche market to promote their product for them by demanding more. It started off slow but then it steadily increased at a strong progressive pace. Their success on this project also reverberated throughout the prison seducing more varied outside interest in the program.

Their first audit sailed along smoothly. But the second one hit a small glitch. Gyps uncovered some international marketeer trying to hack into their product. She handled it quietly and diligently, and the boys continued without any hiccups. However, Gyps and the government continued to maintain an ongoing interest in these poachers for several years.

As each quarter and semester of Eli's study advanced in his studies, the boys upped their ante and expanded their company more into the pacific region. It was a slow progressive advancement and as they did their reputation beheld them as a progressive company that could be trusted. With each improvement Liam developed as well. Within the first year he could talk the talk, walk the walk with the best of them. He was able to translate Eli's cipher into scientific lingo and express it to his customers from his perspective. He was able to express information in both Eli's words and a more advanced technical language. As he became more knowledgeable Liam was no longer the student but a partner in his own right.

His marriage was also proving itself to be the biggest blessing in his life. His adoration for his bride hadn't altered at all but his bride was noticing that Gyps was flirting with her husband. She would often see Gyps watching Liam or sight her laughing with him as they were working. Through her envy and jealousy, she perceived the business relationship between Liam and Gyps as more than a working relationship. She knew that Liam only had eyes for her and didn't see Gyps at all, but Gyp's comfort with her husband made her feel uneasy, suspicious, possessive.

When Liam ventured away to see Eli, his wife took the opportunity to confront Gyps by herself. "Do you have a moment.?"

Gyps thinking it had something to do with work, agreed graciously.

"I don't know how to inform you of this but…. my time is short," she quietly announced, then blatantly accused "and I see you have eyes for my husband."

Gyps was aghast at her accusations. She defended herself quickly "no it's nothing like that" she responded, "I don't think like that." Then with a continued defensive air started explaining.

"You don't understand at all do you?" she exhaled

Liam's bride was now on the defensive.

"It's not your husband I'm admiring, it's his love. His love for you is what I want for me. I see it as information for what to look for, not to take," she defensively explained.

"To be jealous, or envious or to covet someone else's relationship, is to bring that same sourness of relationships upon yourself. You and he are my feedback informing me of the love that has been promised to me. I love watching it. I love watching what I'm going to receive."

"With my husband?" his wife aggravatingly accused.

"No that's coveting. It's not the man, it's the love." Gyps paused as she could Liam's wife was determined to maintain her negative ignorance. "Somewhere out there is someone for me with that same love. By watching and learning I know what to expect, what it looks like, how you both smile all the time, they are things I need to know. I want that for me too and you are both telling me it's in store for me." The reaction of Liam's wife was one of disbelief, as she physically rebuffed Gyp's statement as false.

Gyps stressed even more, "The more I see it, the more I embrace the love you two have for each other, the more I know I will have the same love for me some day. To tear your love apart would manifest the same unbearable pain for me and that can never happen. I would never do that to you but," she emphasised, "I could never do that to me. Please try to understand."

Liam's bride slightly smirked, "so, when I die you will automatically take care of my Li," she paused "is that the plan?" she bitchily narked.

Turning away and ignoring her petty reaction Gyps heartily replied, "Oh, you don't have to worry about him. Gran will take care of him."

"She won't always be there." his wife retorted bluntly. "My Li's world is naive. He needs someone who understands that. Vultures will come and try to take him as a fool. He is a gentle soul, he needs someone who won't …forgive me, but, fuck him over."

Gyps refused to react, but she felt the knife go through her back. This woman wasn't the angel Liam saw in her, and instead of seeing the perfect relationship, Gyps now saw an underlying truth that she would have to recognise within her or experience at a later date.

"No, you're wrong, believe me." she quickly responded. "There are many who will take care of your beautiful man and yes, I will only be one of them who will work with him and they'll all gladly take care of him for you. So, no more worries. You just focus on staying well and being immensely happy as long as you can." she emphasized as she went back to work, hoping the conversation was finished.

However, Liam's bride hadn't finished. Her jealousy now extended to the unknown relationship between Gyps and Gran. She interrogated and questioned not only Gyps but the theories she had heard Liam and Gran talk about, that she never really understood. As Gyps kept on working, she apprehensively agreed to accommodate her and try to explain them

As the boy's first year was coming to an end and the last semester of exams had finished, Eli had handed in all his papers and trajectories, estimations and analysis and had finished all his finals. Liam felt anxious for his brother. He knew Eli understood all his stuff, as he called it, but a lot was riding on their success at this time. When he waltzed in to see Eli, his brother was quite relaxed and comfortable. Liam wasn't expecting this.

Eli wasn't expecting it either. "It's you." he commented. "It's you and Gran," he accusingly declared with a huge grin on his face. Liam had to ask how he came to this conclusion.

"Grans inevitable path shit. It's stuck in my head. This has always been our destiny. All of it." he threw his hand up in acceptance and laughed. "And when you are… are you ready for this?" he said in shock that these words should expel from his mouth. "Gran's famous words, **when you allow,** it all comes to you." Eli laughed at his admissions.

"I studied all I could, handed in all my best papers on time and I know they will be successful, because there's this amazing gut feeling that keeps me calm and says we've got this. It's fucking absurd." He stretched back with his hands on his head.

"The calmness, the stillness, makes you think. When you're crazy like I was, you don't have time to think, or ponder on wisdom, you hate it."

Liam interjected, "but you *lived*. I pondered and thought and life passed me by. This last year has been absolutely chaotic and I've been thinking on my feet, but I'm more alive now than I ever been."

Eli laughed out loud, as he sat forward and met Liam eye to eye. "We've changed places. I'm you and you are me. We're fucked; destiny's fucked?"

Eli quietened down, "the old witch was right, agaaain." Eli raised his eyebrows, "Without every inkling of the fucking manipulation we've lived, we would not be here at this moment. I wouldn't be this calm and confident. We wouldn't be doing this for so many other prisoners. I can't talk about past lives or reincarnation like her, but I do know that without the treachery of our life with our father neither of us would have the resolve to be doing any of this today, fighting for justice, balancing the scales. God knows where we'd be?

I know I wouldn't have this feeling. I know I wouldn't have had the same choices." He leant in close to his brother. "I really want to pass and get a really high score. I've presented some amazing papers through this year, have no idea where all the ingenuity came from, it was automatic, and my last one I presented today was fucking awesome. When we pass, hundreds will follow in our shoes. Do you realise that?" He bit his mouth.

"I've always known that this day would come, but today is D-Day and the realisation of what we have done has just hit home. I seriously believe we succeeded." Eli started laughing, "That's phenomenal," he laughed, "we did that. I've never dreamed that big for me in my entire life. The old witch was right, the dream comes to you. I just did what I loved most and it all came flowing to me."

Liam sat back and listened as Eli continued. It was as if destiny had hold of his tongue and wasn't going to shut up, "I don't know how fate works but it seems to mean that if dad's path and mine didn't cross the way that it did, none of these guys would be free. Does that make sense? Crazy. So, by eliminating him or the shit he represented as the witch would say, they will all be saved or some stupid thing. Too deep for me, but it's happening all around me."

"You're right," responded Liam with a very stern voice. Then he paused, "You do sound like Gran." Then he cracked up laughing.

When they settled Liam remembered one more of her inspirational quotations, "it's the maths you have to look at." He whispered as he continued "What is it? Opposite and equal value."

Then Eli sat upright "no, it's the other one. I thought of it today, the opposite and equal is when you're fighting and reacting it's the karmic one. I'm talking about the freedom one. The revolutionary one not the evolutionary one. The one where if you come from freedom and equality, you create more fuckin freedom and that's what we did. That's what we fuckin did. We altered the laws. We created new laws. Now instead of opposites being attracted to us to test us, we attract like to us and all evolve together," He paused and saw the look of disbelief on Liam's face. "Yeah, I listened."

Still completely amazed at the years events, Eli commented "All her unbelievable reincarnational bull, happened for real for both of us. Once a witch, always a witch. Where did she learn all that stuff anyway?" he mumbled.

Liam sat back in fascinated wonder, "Wow where did my brother go? I came here today worried about you and your exams and this is what I get; totally not what I expected. If I didn't know better, I say you're drunk."

Eli interrupted, "Have a drink for me tonight. I feel incredibly successful and somehow all that shit she talked about, has a lot to do with it. All her stupid rabble is changing me as I'm getting older. They're not attached to any religion or belief system which to me was just another establishment.

I think that is why I hated her bunk as a kid I thought it was a religion. But this shit is back to front man. I did what I loved first; then her rabble that's stuck in my head says, 'see that's how ya do it; now do it again.'

Liam burst out laughing for this was another first for him. Now they could converse together on a more controversial level. It was no longer what 'Gran said' but what they had accomplished together because of what Gran taught.

Eli couldn't stop rambling. Liam joined in spasmodically but Eli mostly had the floor. Liam then questioned about their new path and the advancement they hoped to achieve next year. An over excited Eli went to his room and returned with a file with new ideas and prospects he wanted to experiment.

Now Liam could physically see the thrill and excitement exuding from Eli as he exposed three new exhilarating possible future directions that could prove to be extremely rewarding for all parties. "Got the guts to do a Walt Disney?" he dared Liam with a huge smile on his face. Liam nowunderstood Eli's enthusiasm and nodded eagerly as they both put their heads together and started to analyzed all their options.

Liam was so enthralled by these new innovative proposals that he totally forgot about the time. He had to rush home. He had a beautiful wife at there waiting for him.

When he arrived home his beautiful wife and Gyps were enjoying a bottle of fine wine and some silly show on the new screen in the lounge. Liam stood the door with a grin, "miss me?"

Up popped his very tipsy wife. "Always darling," as she kissed him sensually on the lips. She returned to her seat and smirked at Gyps as the winner.

"Have I missed something?"

"Oh, you have no idea darling," stated his little bit drunk wife. "Did you know the world isn't flat it's round and you won't fall off the edge after all. Isn't that exciting. Oh god I'm drunk." She held her head. "Shouldn't have moved."

"I'll let myself out," stated Gyps quietly as she gathered her jacket and started to leave, "I think she needs you more than me right now."

"Thank you." Liam knelt beside his lovely wife, "I've never seen you drunk before," he giggled as he checked out the empty wine bottle.

"Am I pretty," she slurred.

"Divine."

With that response, she then proceeded to projectile all over him. As he found his dignity, he realised his lovely wife just christened their brand-new carpet. He helped her to her feet and knew he would be in for a hard trek to the back of the house. He couldn't take her to their bedroom upstairs, it had champagne carpet and no, he wasn't going to risk that. He would settle her and return with some soda water and hoped he could rescue the grey carpet from the red puddle that imbued the centre of the floor in a perfect circular formation.

Somehow this day simply wasn't going to plan at all. He was hoping to share adrink with his wife and celebrate their victory but she had her own victory to celebrate. "Yep, my darling, the world is definitely round. Big discovery."

He tidied up the room and had a shower then snuggled in beside the love of his life. Even drunk she was unbelievably precious to him. I'll make her breakfast in bed tomorrow I don't think she'll be able to. Still a year of firsts.

New learning curve tomorrow; how does my wife wake up with a hangover? He snuggled into her and fell asleep.

"Tomorrow we start again, round two"

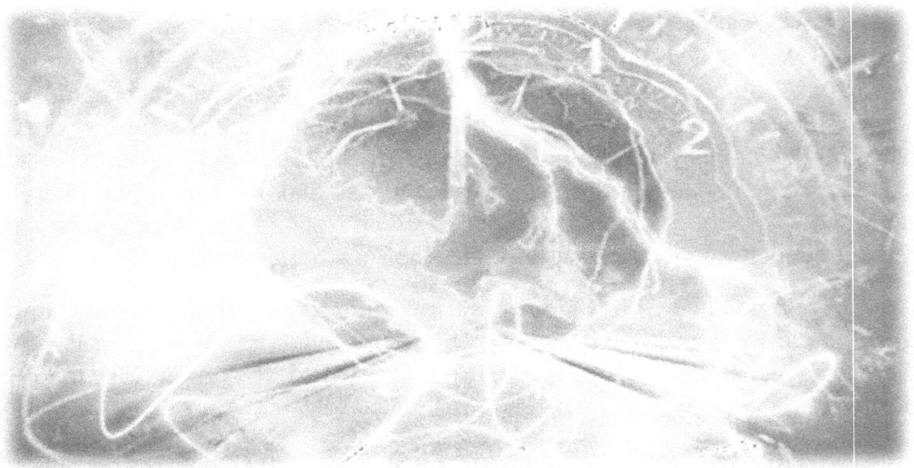

CHAPTER EIGHTEEN

ANOTHER YEAR; ANOTHER YEAR:

Due to Eli's extraordinary creativity and his computerised ingenuity in their international business eventually Liam had to relinquish his career as a scientist. As the years passed their monumental achievements kept generating more productivity and success beyond belief for both boys and the prison program. The chairman and the boys engineered a program to include more beneficial options for the prison and more apprentices. Once Eli completed his PhD's he became more involved in the prison's rehabilitation apprenticeship program, using their import business as the foundation stone.

The original program was established for mature students but now it incorporated young and old lads as well. Eli formed together a team of successful applicants as marketeers who'd proven to be successful to work with him in finding more contracts for prisoners for suitable apprenticeships. They would then interview the different prospects and synchronise all of them in suitable positions.

It all ran like a well-oiled machine. The chairman and Eli answered to the training board tribunal and the government sections for further trade and education. When the time came for the chairman to retire, a female regulator stepped into his position. She showed even more enthusiasm for the apprenticeship program. She wanted more equality for women prisoners as well. So, she instigated a training program where the brilliance of the men's scheme was created where both male and female prisons collaborated together.

She believed there wasn't male and female apprenticeships they were all simply University Apprenticeships.

This opened up variable new doors to male hairdressers and female engineers. Now the apprenticeship scheme had taken on an entirely new expansive format. Not only integrating prison programs, but also national apprenticeships. What this meant was that when a prisoner was released, they had a self-sufficient career in their home town thousands of kilometres away. What it also did was it gave the prisoner personal value which prevented them from wanting to return.

Eli woke up every morning and within the prison walls he went to work. He loved his job and he love what he was doing at no time did he regret that he was still in prison. This feeling of autonomy within him made him feel completely free. As he aged, he would hear himself wafting out his Gran's ethos to this teams and giving them inspiration to be better than their environment.

Years passed as the quarter of a century confinement came to a finish and Eli found himself facing his final year. It was like his senior year at school. He had achieved so much and he really didn't want to leave. He, like all the apprentices, was self-sufficient outside, he had his business with his brother; a huge house to return to; however, it was like stepping back into his past.

There were board meetings and approvals followed by the final parole board of judgement.

Eli sat across the table awaiting their questions. They read his approval ratings from both chairmen. They read his report of the work and achievements he had accomplished during his time in prison. They totally disregarded all of them. He was a murderer, he was imprisoned, restricted, he had to behave like this, but had he been rehabilitated enough to adjust to the real world.

They were a callous, cold group of people who had their own opinions of his actions twenty-five years ago. They all still saw him as THAT murderer. Eli hadn't been treated with such denigration by anyone in over 20 years.

Do you regret killing you father?

Would you do it again?

What would you say to that boy now?

He told them all the answers they wanted to hear, for they would not want to hear the truth. No, he will not kill again for that would destroy his life not anyone else's. His views on his father would no concur with theirs.

And what would he tell himself. Freedom is a choice, but they wouldn't understand that either for at the very table where they sat and judged him, they deliberately tried to victimise and re-incriminate him, take his freedom from him.

They put him in their incarcerated box and accused him from their…. what did the old chairman used to call them; yes, "their goody two shoes, perspective."

When he exited the interrogation room, he felt the wretchedness within him again. He recognised the incarcerating feelings enclosing in on him like a weed. He whispered to himself, 'the opinions of others define you.' then he made up his own adage, don't allow the opinions of others to destroy your freedom."

Within days his release paper were signed. Eli laughed; "Now it's legit," Freedom was never about walking out the gates of the prison.

Freedom was knowing that the prison gates didn't really exist. However, his world was bigger on the inside of prison than it would ever be on the outside.

As Eli exited the prison for the last time, he was met by an old man. He saw his brother in the natural light for the first time in over 25 years. Liam had aged but then so had Eli. He refused to look back at the doors as he heard them close behind him. He had spent over half his life cocooned in that establishment now he needed to see how if world he used to live in had altered.

Liam brother embraced him so tightly and didn't want to let him go. He was well widowed now. His wife finally passed after six years of marriage. Their life together was happy and he doesn't regret any moment of it. He escorted his baby brother to an Aston Martin in the car park. Liam smirked as he threw Eli the keys. "This is yours. Can you still remember how to drive them?"

"We had vehicles inside, not as nice as this lady though. Wow, even she's grown. Not like the baby I had. Have the road rules changed?" Liam shook his head. "Then let's see what she's got."

They cruised nicely along an open road Eli didn't recognise. Eli had spent 25 years in this area and had no idea what it really looked like. It was nothing but vacant dry land and pastures. They could have walked out anytime and no one would have found them. Amazing how so much emptiness can keep you confined.

After half an hour of driving they came across their first town, and Eli was tempted to stop but changed his mind. Liam wanted to know why?

"I suspect many a newly released prisoner would stop here and I can feel the prejudice just in looking at the town." Liam was surprised, Eli wasn't like this. Something had happened. Eli drove and talked and laughed but he remained clammed.

Liam told him to take a turn right and start heading for the bay area. "I've decided to sell the business to our uncle and start again," commented Liam. Before Eli could lose his cool, Liam butted in and said, "Will you trust me on this please."

 Eli felt betrayed, "we can make 10 million a year from that business, easy, that was going to be my future now what?" He waited then reacted, "Why? Couldn't we have at least talked about it first?"

"That was your prison job. New start, new life. Besides I have a surprise for you." Liam smiled like the Cheshire cat.

They drove to a cafe in the bay where their uncle was waiting for the papers. "You're selling it to him?" Liam went in alone and advised his brother to remain in the car. He and his uncle signed the deeds, then Liam returned with a cheque for $30 million dollars.

As he climbed back into the car, and he handed Eli the cheque. "It is worth far more than that," responded Eli. Eli glanced up and saw his uncle maliciously waving the deeds to the business in the window indicting to Eli, he had finally won.

"The dock my man," requested Liam as he pointed in the northern direction. As soon as they arrived the boys were met by chauffeurs who were ready to drive the car to the docking bay. Eli reluctantly gave him the keys as Liam took another set out of his pocket. "You'll need these now. Catch."

As Eli caught the keys. Liam pointed to a double storey yacht called "The Eliam." Eli's dream baby; a yacht, double deck, faster than lightning, and it was finally his. He'd been dreaming of a beautiful baby like this since he was a boy.

Sailing was all Eli ever wanted to do, but no one heard him. But now he realised someone was listening. Liam always heard him.

They walked closer to the mooring and on board the yacht was a tall leggy female in shorts and a mariners T-shirt. "That is your First Mate." grinned Liam. "Mediterranean sailing and yachtsman champion. I figured if you really want to learn how to handle this baby, get the best."

A chubby gentleman stood at the bottom of the plank, "this is your chef," stated Liam. Beside him was a fragment of a female manipulating her father to let her join the cruise. Then she sexually flashed her eyes at Eli "I could be very good."

Eli stared at the father and without flinching, "She stays; I don't do victim." Then he walked up the plank to his lounge. "Welcome aboard sir," responded his First Mate. Liam followed up behind him. He received a salute and "Captain." Eli looked back at him, and mimicked "Captain?" then he patronisingly smirked.

As they pulled out Liam joined Eli at the bar in the lounge. "Okay what's going on?" Eli tried to wave it off but Liam was having no part of it. Liam stayed on the stool while Eli sprawled himself out on the plush lounge.

Eli thought awhile, then deduced, "I was taught freedom in that place. We introduced a program in that place so that when prisoners both male and female were released, they won't want to return. They'll be an accepted part of society. Total bullshit," he furiously rebutted. He quietly sulked for a minute, then sat upright.

"I went to that parole board meeting and for the first time in over 20 years those people looked at me and accused me of being a murderer. That's all they could see. All that work, all that rehabilitation for nothing. They read my paperwork, they read my achievements and totally ignored all of them giving precedence to a murder charge from 25 years ago."

Liam went to interrupt but Eli yelled "it's not us; it's them; they're the reason prisoners keep wanting to return. They're the reason all these programs are for nothing. We've done all the rehabilitating, we've changed, we've developed, we've grown, and they, these pompous asses who deem themselves better than us because of their houses and positions, haven't changed at all.

They are still the same unyielding judgemental bastards from years ago. You saw your uncle; they don't give you a chance. In the real world we are accused, victimised and imprisoned forever but in prison we are taught to be free; what the fuck for?"

Liam picked up the bottle and took it over to replenish his brother's glass. He smiled at him "so that you can tell a sassy little cook's daughter, you don't do victim," Liam laughed.

"Gran's expression," answered Eli but he didn't want any words of wisdom at that moment, however that didn't stop Liam. "You have to experience all that it isn't."

Eli completed the quote reluctantly with a nod. "To know what it is, yeah."

Liam raised his glass to his brother "And as much as I hate to say it brother dear, you now fucking know." argued Liam and Eli reciprocated.

Feeling totally pissed off Eli reacted, "Twenty-five years to return to this," as he threw up his arms up in dismay then looking around him, Eli had to ask how Liam could afford such a yacht. "Sold the house." Liam smiled like a cat that caught the mouse.

"With all the upgrades and renos we transformed that place from dad's shitbox to a place of extreme computerised technical brilliance in every room. The outside looked like a simple home but inside was a Sci-Fi's fantasy. The house did it all for you. But it just wasn't the same."

Eli reacted "Sorry about your wife, really Liam, regardless of her rubbish." Liam nonchalantly responded that they got more time than they expected and it was good while it lasted.

Changing the subject Liam enthusiastically explained "Follow the dream, well, I got an outrageous offer for the house, from one of our Pacific Consortiums, then this beauty magically came on the market, nudge, nudge, wink, wink and I thought why not? You were getting out soon and I knew you loved sailing and all fell into place as you say." As the afternoon drew to a close, they sipped a few more scotches then, Eli found his way to a main bedroom.

Soft huge queen bed, large double wardrobe filled with a variety of clothes, a personal shower, scented shaving gear, shampoo and deodorant that was all his own. Fresh soft towels and he relished all of it.

After his shower, he went up on board to the helm and stood beside the sweetest smelling First Mate anyone could ever ask for. He felt like a new man again. It was as if the shower had finally washed nearly thirty years of shit away. He stood still just absorbing the gush of air that belted against his body. This was freedom at its best. "Where to?" he asked.

She pointed to the navigational radar. "Gran's resort?" Eli yelled out to his brother below, "you're taking me to Gran's resort?" He raised his eye brows "I'm out of prison and that's the best you've got? Haven't you heard of the Caribbean, the Rivera, fuck the north pole, but Gran's resort really?"

"We've got some business there." echoed the laughing response back to him.

He started conversing with his First Mate as she held the helm steadily. "You want to try sir," she asked? "She's as smooth as an Astin Martin, only with more balls." She explained all the fancy attachments in basic English then let him have total control of the vessel. "This lady does it all for you only with dignity," she concluded.

As he took wheel, he felt the delicate but immense power of the vessel he was steering. "I love this. This is sailing. You enjoy sailing?" he asked her politely.

She laughed sarcastically, "this is yachting sir. This lady does it all for you. You don't have to think, guide or react. You don't even have to know the currents, the tides or water breaks. It's all computerised for you and your yacht determines the action to be taken. This is like Soft more's guide to gardening." Eli waited for the resolution. "Hire a gardener sir." He laughed.

She pulled out her wallet, flipped it open, and with gushing pride, "that's sailing sir. She's my baby Genoa." With pride in her voice and eyes she gushed, "many a race won and lost in her because you, not your computer, you have to know your wind, current, sails. You and your lady have to be one and your success at any regatta depends entirely on your ability to sail, not the yachts."

Eli glanced at the image, "Teach me," pleaded Eli. "Teach me that. I want to be your First Mate. I want to know how to sail; Teach me? You're right, this is fun, but that," a huge passionate smile of enthusiasm engulfed his face. He nodded to himself, "that would be awesome."

His First Mate stated it would take years, to which Eli responded, "I've got years."

"I'm in training for I've got another race in two months and we need some renos on her but with a good sponsor she'll be up and cruising in no time. That's why I'm doing this stint. Your brother has offered me really good money to navigate this girl so I took the job and now I'll have my girl ready for the titles. She pointed to the navigational system, "watch your sights."

"How did you know that?" Eli asked. You didn't look at the system before you told me I was out, you knew I was, how did you know," Eli queried with anticipation

"Sailing alone for years, I guess. The currents, the winds, tides, it's all information. You learn to read it." She smiled at the peculiar look on his face. "I'll sponsor you…. I'll sponsor you and you teach me how to sail. What do you say to that?"

"Oh, I wasn't manipulating you into sponsoring me please." she pleaded that he understand "I will get a sponsor."

"You have one," he smirked. "I have no life now, I'm re-starting again, and this has always been my ultimate dream forever. And if sponsoring you is my means to achieving that then it makes every stinkin' part of it was worthwhile. Now tell me more. This is like my bestest, most favourite bedtime story ever. Indulge me…. please?"

She laughed at his terminology. "Really?" He echoed her. As she spoke, he nurtured every word as if they were building blocks to the new Eli.

"It's coming into dark. We'll be pulling into that bay in about half an hour away and dropping anchor there. We'll set sail again early in the morning, little after sunrise and be at your Grans by noon. Do you want me to dock her?"

He shook his head, "she's my lady, teach me. Then I'll take you to the dining room for dinner. We've got a lot to talk about," he flirtatiously smirked.

Eli and his First Mate sat at a corner table enjoying a romantic dinner while Liam enjoyed the company of the chef.

When morning came Liam chanced upon the First Mate exiting Eli's room in his shirt and heading for the shower. That wasn't on the agenda but it certainly was long overdue.

Breakfast was finished and swiftly the yacht was underway again, and all faces were aglow. For the next six hours Eli was trained and informed by his First Mate of all he needed to know to man his yacht completely on his own. He took his instructions seriously and when his First Mate took the helm, he stood behind her, slipped his arm around her and sailed the yacht with her. His ultimate dream; She smelt so good and the yacht felt so good, this was how he envisaged himself spending the rest of his life.

His First Mate talked his talk, talked his dreams and he wanted to walk with her for as long as he could. Liam was right. When we find the right one, or the one we want to be right, we become so blinded with total tunnel vision we see no other.

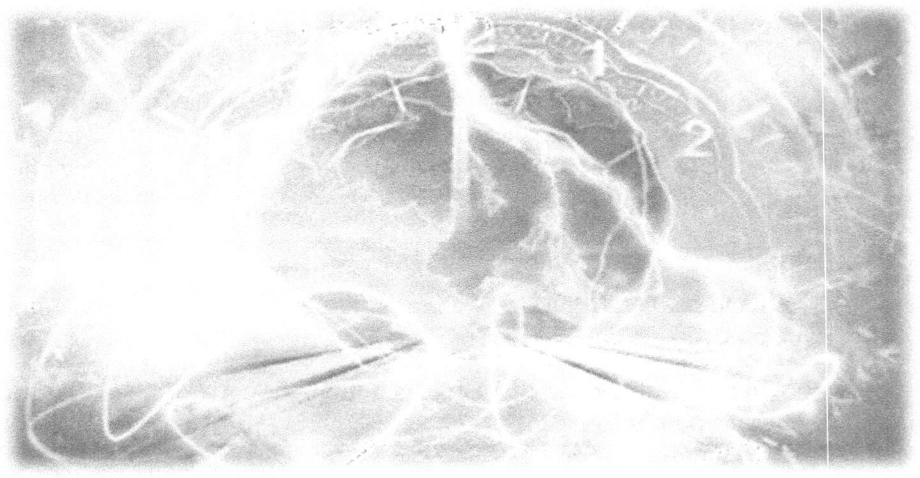

CHAPTER NINETEEN

STARTING AGAIN; AGAIN.

The ELIAM docked at an exclusive island resort mooring. There was welcoming committee who came and greeted all of them. "Your rooms are waiting," responded the concierge. "We will bring your bags."

"Whoa, this is not how I remembered this place at all," reacted Eli as they walked up the cleanly paved path to the exclusive residence.

"No, we've grown extensively," came a remark echoing from behind them as a familiar voice resounded to both Eli and Liam. Liam was excitedly taken back as he greeted Gyps and Eli introduced her to his First Mate. Gyps very efficiently took control of the situation, "Please gentlemen, and lady, this way, your things will be taken to your rooms and if you require anything else just ask, everything is compliments of the house."

She allowed them to sign in, then when they were ready, she escorted all of them back outside to the more exclusive recluse area of the resort. It was set up as the private lounge area for conferences, meetings and management, surrounded by local floral and attended by a personal bartender.

As they walked in, they were all handed a glass of scotch and ushered to their specific seats of comfort. Liam commented, "one of ours." Eli had tasted their selections but never allowed to indulge. As he tasted their merchandise he was extremely impressed at the uniqueness and smoothness of the drop.

The three of them chatted among themselves then finally in walked their grand matriarch and owner. She immediately walked over to Liam open armed and gave him a huge hug. Then she turned to Eli, "You got a hug for your old witch?" Eli laughed as he stood up and embraced his Gran whole heartedly, with a smile, he whispered in her ear, "thank you." Eli then turned introduced her to his First Mate. "Welcome child."

Gran received her drink and sat comfortably in her wicca peacock chair and swiftly got down to business. "Down to business; There's a lot of stuff to cover so let's start. Due to the belatedness of the situation you have to sign these papers immediately. I've held on to them long enough. They are your inheritance."

Both men were perplexed by the comment. They didn't want their Grans money yet. She paused for a moment. She knew this day would come and she always thought she was ready for it, but as always, this moment took her breath away.

'It's your mothers." She watched Eli as he rebuked the idea of having anything that belonged to her. As he was about to exercise his objectionable opinion, in walked a tall aged man, both boys recognised and were shocked to see, especially here at this resort and under these conditions; the chairman.

Eli mimed, "What the fuck?"

The chairman straddled to a seat that was waiting for his presence.He too was presented with his scotch as he sat in his peacock seat beside Gran,he placed his drink on the centre table, "I promised her I'd take care of you."he responded.

There was a long pause, Liam sat gob smacked, figuring out the maths while Eli indignantly reacted, "What, before she abandoned us and bumped herself off." He shook his head in disgust.

The chairman took his drink and had a straight swig beckoning for another. "She was my daughter." declared the chairman. Now that he got that off his chest, he stared at the boys watching their every reaction as he started telling the truth about the death of his grandchildren's mother.

He waited for silence, "I ran an importing business much like yours and mine was quite successful too back then." The boy's ears pricked as this story was known to them. "It was a time when all this was new so to find someone who was making a profit from it was extraordinary." As he received his second drink he continued.

"Word got round that your father wanted me to join forces with him but I didn't need him, in fact he would have been a loose cannon. He underhandedly married my daughter, and started using her as leverage. I still refused and he started belting and abusing her. The plan was for us to get her out of there before he killed her and then come back for you boys as soon as we could. Your mother objected but when she wound up in hospital inches from death from one of his beatings, she had no choice, I simply took her.

Your father then took out a restraining order against her saying she was the abusive parent and you children were the victims. He won. So, we then took out a counter order and accused him and with the proven evidence from her and the fact that you children would tell the truth. We were coming back for you. We knew with you," he pointed to Eli, "we would win."

Gran interjected again. "Unfortunately, your mother secretly met with your aunt. She wanted to know if you boys were safe. The bitch betrayed all of you. They got a 2-million-dollar house, a share in your father's business and future security for their children and you lost," she paused as a tear came to her eye and she again gasped for breath, "you lost your mother."

Eli was shaking his head back and forth in total disbelief. The chairman continued, "Your father would have lost everything. He couldn't have that, so he and his brother, killed her. He orchestrated it; his brother took care of it." The chairman sipped more of his drink and before replacing it on the table he painfully continued, "Make it look like an accident, and he did."

He sat back comfortably in his peacock seat crossed his legs, and referring to Eli, "Only like you son, the witnesses you don't expect. He came to me. I wanted to murder the bastards there and then but then your Gran pleaded with me and won.

My parents died when I was very young and I spent most of my time in abhorrent foster care. Your Gran reminded me of that. If I killed them, you boys would have been, well we'd have never seen either of you again; this way at least we could keep you reasonably safe."

"Safe? I murdered my father," blasted Eli as he stood up in total disgust of the entire situation. "He told me, she left me, she didn't want me, she didn't want us." He started weeping. Liam jumped up and grabbed him and they held each other tightly, until the pain subsided.

"Oh, my darlings, he lied; he always lied," responded Gran lovingly. "She loved you boys so much. You were her entire world. She was coming back for you; We were coming back for you. You were her first thought of a morning and her last thought of a night and I dare say, her last thoughts."

The chairman butted in, "As for wanting to kill your father, there were a lot of people in line. You just got in first; jeopardizing your own safety. You gave your uncle's family everything they wanted, now you were the loose cannon, Gran and I knew that, so we initiated some precautionary measures."

Liam sat mumbling to himself, "All this time I just thought they were unforgiving pricks but they were," he paused and reticently responded, "I thoughtlessly kept putting you in danger. You knew?"

Without saying a word, he indicated his knowledge of the danger he was in. Gyps interrupted from her indiscreet corner. "We always had your back, both of you."

"Is that why you worked at the prison?" Liam asked the chairman.

"No. No I seriously wanted changes in the system. But I did make arrangements to have Eli placed in my jurisdiction. Then when I heard that you wanted to return to university and I had heard about the apprenticeship scheme, I wanted you to be so successful at it that you wouldn't need your uncle's business. I knew you weren't a murderer, none of those guys were, but when you showed your potential, that was your mother all over again. So many times I wanted to hug you two boys and congratulate you two boys but that would have destroyed everything. So now we are almost done." The young men reclaimed their seats and decided to look over the papers. Both men looked up in amazement.

"Yes, you are both quite wealthy men now in your own right. Your mother's parents in Europe were extremely wealthy and they left everything to you, almost as a reward. As I said there were a lot of people in line."

The chairman questioned Liam "You made your uncle sign for the importing business." Liam nodded and agreed he did everything as requested. "Good." Their grandfather smiled.

"What are you up to?" questioned Eli "I know that look. I've seen that look before."

The old man smiled, "For forty years I have wanted that bastard. In one of our many talks your Gran said there is a better way, and we had to be patient, so I waited and she was right. When we set up the computer system our major concern was hackers. We did everything we could to prevent even the slightest trepidation. One almost broke through.

 Liam, he used your private contact to your other European concerns that only your family knew about. That's what caught him out; he knew your private name as well as your username. We knew it was him or connected to him from the start. We locked him out but watched him for twenty odd years.

Liam started questioning how because he saw nothing to indicate any abnormalities. In the corner discretely sat Gyps with a smirk on her face, "told you not to worry."

"That's why I trust her completely. Your Gran and I wanted both of you boys safe before we allowed all the concerned parties to have all the information they needed, to have all their dreams come true and to hang all the bastards at the same time. So, either our government will get them and absolutely fry them or your Asian consortium will have him vanish and take over their little empire. That arse thinks he's so smart, but his greed will grant him his death wish or at least mine."

"Nearly forty years you've been sitting on this," queried Liam, "forty years quietly stewing. And I thought my biggest shock today was that you two knew each other."

Eli peered at Liam, astoundingly gagging and nodding and pointing his finger at both of the oldies, "Yeah me too. Do you know how many times I said, oh you should meet my Gran, what the?" they all started laughing,"geez."

"Well, there's more my darlings." stated Gran as she again wanted the floor. She started indicating to the chairman and herself "we decided to tie the knot. We've known each other for years and thought there's no time like the present."

Eli joshed and laughed at the humour of it all, "You're married?" and as he laughed out loud, he sarcastically asked, "Wow, what do we call you?"

Gran took Eli's hand and mockingly whispered in his ear, "the Pirate and the witch," she winked. "He knew quite a lot about the black market back then too."

Eli loved her new found humour with his humour, then in astonishment, "He's the Pirate?" he pointed to the chairman and repeated, "You're the Pirate? Dad hated you, he wanted you dead, you were his nemesis and you were his father-in-law?" He glanced at Liam, "Told ya, fucked in the head, all of 'em." He was becoming overwhelmed by all these confessions. "This just keeps getting better."

Eli indicated to the barman his need for a refill "Leave the bottle, there's not enough booze in the world today for all this bullshit." Eli started scratching his head in total disbelief of the day's unfolding's. This was a holocaust of a homecoming. Every belief he built his life on has just been shattered in front of him. His entire life has been a complete fiasco.

"I've put the resort in new and very accomplished hands, while we go to Europe, lay low for a while. Although we see it as finally finishing, we don't want to get caught up in the loose ends. Suggest you do the same."

Gran gazed at Eli questionly. He responded, "clean slate." Then he tipped his glass to her, Gran reciprocated.

"This is my new manager," she said that she indicated to Gyps in the corner. Gyps nodded at the introduction. With hand gestures Liam queried the connection between the three of them.

Feeling much more relaxed now, the chairman explained, "Gyps has always been my business manager and offsider. When I started working with you lads I introduced to Gyps to your Gran's and she became her business advisor as well.

Your wife ideas were responsible for all the major upgrades here. Her communication contacts took this place virtually from the old resort to this technological monstrosity and Gyps has been the one transforming the place to OTB and it has been a massive success ever since. But we kept this week free from all the usual resort bustle for you boys, your home coming son."

"OTB why OTB," questioned Liam.

The chairman raised his glass, and pondered for a moment, "Maybe you should know it all. Maybe you should know Eli just how much we do love you and the lengths we went to save you boys." He looked at Gran for concurrence and she sat back relaxed and nodded.

Eli and Liam were so flabbergasted at the day's events so far, through their frustration they both agreed, all they could say was "bring it on."

The chairman whispered to Gyps to retrieve something for him and she quietly retreated. He prepared himself and began. "Fill your glasses men. Eli, I'm your grandfather, and when I heard you killed that brute, I was pissed with your Gran for not letting me take care of him years before. That was when your Gran shouted me to some of her scotch and interesting philosophies. What you boys don't know is Gyps is more eccentric than your Gran so I was bombarded from both sides," he laughed.

By killing your father, you opened a lot of very happy doors, but you also shut a lot of doors. The shut ones wanted you dead but the opened ones we all started working together against your opposition without harming you boys.

When you were sentenced, they, as in your uncle's business family, paid your lawyers to have you placed, in Burnside. You would been taken care of there." Liam reacted in disbelief but Eli acted as if he knew. "Gran approached me and asked for help, so I organised for you to be transferred to my rehabilitation centre.

Gyps, and a few phone calls, a few favours and we got you out of their clutches at Burnside. You wouldn't have survived. When we succeeded, Gran introduced me to *This* bottle of scotch to celebrate. It was the smoothest

Scotch I had ever tasted. We toasted and she said *"only the best,"* and from that day on, that's what we decided to do.

Somehow, we would provide both you boys with only the best that life could offer even if you were incarcerated. You would both now be free of their clutches for life.

Then you both asked about the uni exercise and Liam, because you wanted out of their business, your uncles' lawyers panicked and orchestrated some misappropriations to take place within the center causing Eli's to have a fatal accident. Your personal guard," Eli questioned that comment, "Yes, he was your personal body guard; he got wind of it so we upgraded you to the other side of the facility out of their sight."

Eli nodded, "I remember that; but I never thought for a moment that was the reason though. They got that close," he breathed a sigh, "far out."

The chairman added, "That's why Gyps recommended your guard go with you to your brother's wedding. The minute she said it I knew what she meant."

Liam caught Gyp's glance and smiled.

"We also thought they'd go after you Liam, so we again called in some favours, we had someone talk to your father's lawyers and let it slip that you boys would now be working international imports with the Government, hence they were more than happy to sell it to you and we were able to keep both of you safe for a little longer."

Liam commented with a sigh, "Thought it felt too easy." He tipped his glass to Gyps. She grinned.

Eli then suddenly turned sombre, then jumped on the bandwagon, "So you've controlled all of this?"

The chairman interjected quickly, "Oh I see what you're going with that, no. Your success on that project for the apprenticeships, was awe inspiring."

With a huge proud smile on his face, the chairman explained. "That was when I wanted to grab both you boys and hug you and scream 'THESE ARE MY DAUGHTER'S BOYS.' I wanted to tell you both then how much you were like your mother, but that would have destroyed everything we were all trying to achieve."

The chairman's audience now curiously allowed him to continue. "The first year the tribunal seriously questioned your work. It was extraordinary. They thought you cheated or conspired with someone or we helped you; they didn't believe it was your work. Your body guard, while you two were having a visitation, borrowed your drafts and presented them to the tribunal. Some dead shits were still skeptical, but the ones who understood it, the ones who comprehended how you reached your results, well Eli they were inspired, they wanted more. Then for the next three next years, well, both of you went ballistic.

Eli cracked up laughing; "Our Walt Disney years; they were fun."

As those words caught the Chairman's attention, he proudly mimed, "of course."

"You created brand new unknown apps, markets and market strategies that the no man including the tribunal had never seen before. They had to agree that you were a dynamo and that without the apprenticeship you may never have reached your full potential. Some of them also saw it as an opportunity.

Those first few years of your creative ingenuity cemented the future scholarships for thousands of individuals within the prison. It also cemented some of the tribunal members as well, they supported and instigated many of your strategies and became profitable markets in their own rights. And that's the next point of interest we want to show to you boys; Gran?" she nodded. Cheer's boys, Another round here please."

Gyps returned and placed a file on the table in front of Gran. The chairman could now continue. "We, as in your Gran and I went POA and copyrighted three of your ingenious computer marketing apps, and they now are still part of industries best. These are your registered papers. Your gran and I have signed them over to you and had them witnessed by your lawyer. Congratulation's boys," he raised his glass.

As Eli scanned the papers, he processed what they had accomplished, "achieve the unachievable."

Holding his glass in his hand the chairman stated, "Now every time we toast with this scotch, it's for all of us, forever. New paths, new futures, futures that are derived from, what did you call it? Old Walt Disney? That's us achieving the unachievable. To all of us, altogether, forever, only the best. We no longer do shit, we do freedom, that's us." he raised his glass and swilled every last drop.

Gran had to ask curiously, "Why did you call it Walt Disney?"

Eli answered with a surprised grin, "it's your story Gran, achieving the unachievable."

With a look of surprise on her face Gran retorted, "That was your mother's story, not mine. O my lord, you remember that?" she queried.

The chairman smiled as he recalled, "I taught her that when she was little."

She relaxed as she expressed with a smile, "Now it all makes sense." They all scanned each other as Gran had her epiphany. "I could never see it before but now I see it, that darling girl."

All her audience wanted to understand her revelation as well or at least hear it.

"Now I understand why she had to leave when she did. It was for you boys. If she stayed your father would have erased all that hope she imprinted on your DNA from her and both of you like a vacuum. But by leaving when she did, he couldn't touch it, making it still available for you when you wanted it, but you still had to choose. Once you chose you activated those codes those feelings, then there was no stopping you. I know I'm rambling but it makes sense to me."

"No Gran," interrupted Eli. "I used to think even comment to Liam that you were haunting me," they laughed, "but you're saying it was mum."

"No darling she wasn't haunting you, that's impossible, I think, but her DNA meaning all of her beliefs were a part of your DNA, all of them. The reason she got mixed up with your father's abhorrent life was because of you two boys, not your father. That's what I couldn't understand, how such a beautiful woman like her could get involved with such a violent brute like him, it didn't make sense. But she wasn't following him she was following you two. She was showing you who you boys were before you got caught up in centuries of his brutal narcissism. Her beliefs have always been within both of you, but neither of you could reactivate it until you eliminated the obstacle that was preventing it."

The boys looked in horror at her words, "not your father, he was also showing you the obstacle in you that was preventing you from returning to your original path. As I always said, this entire course was Karmic Justice, not justice."

There was a stilled silence as the boys and the chairman absorbed her words as she unraveled and healed the reasons for their loss. Gran apologized for putting a damper on Eli's home coming.

"Gran I never analyzed it, I just did it, but now," with a sensitive smirk on his face "understanding all this bull, that's what I'm going to do." He paused with a huge grin of condescension on his face,

"Well, you have a choice, that bullshit or this bullshit; just a matter of which paddock you want to play in." Eli enjoyed his humorous inspiration.

Suddenly there was light in Eli's eyes and a fire in his belly. "You," He pointed at the chairman.

You missed something. You do free us; we can fly; inside… But these bags of bones," referring to the outside world, "want to keep us incarcerated. You and the staff in there, never looked at us as prisoners or murderers. You made sure everyone there was treated with respect, as a person. You just forgot to tell the parole board and the people on the outside.

Those mercenary, cold hearted bastards convicted me all over again. Then when I came outside those doors and was physically free, I felt victimised all over again. We are free, in there, that's why we keep wanting to return. Out here it's victim against victim. They're the ones who are imprisoned, and somehow I have to continue what you started, but I'll prepare them for this pile of crap." Then he looked flirtingly at his First Mate, "first you're going to teach me how to sail like a champion, and we'll do that around the world then we'll kick fundamentalists arses, what do you say?"

Liam responded, "that sounded like a proposal," Eli glanced back at his brother accusingly.

Liam responded, "Hey, we fall quickly and we fall hard. And we never see anyone else and we have the best of times. What can I say?"

Eli quietly said as he gazed into his first mate's eyes "It's not that I can't look at another woman, I simply don't want to." He smiled. He shrugged his shoulders.

Eli started standing up readying himself to leave. "That's what we do man," he retorted. "Love walks in one door and our eyesight go out the other. Totally blind forever unless someone wakes us up; otherwise, completely doomed," and as he said that he bent down and gently kissed his First Mate on the lips. "See you at dinner?" he shook his head and shrugged his shoulders as if he was a lost cause. "You've won me." He handed his glass back to the waiter as he walked to his room to change for dinner.

"Did you come prepared for dinner dear?" asked Gran. The First Mate shook her head. Gran beckoned to Gyps "Could you assist this young lass with some appropriate attire for dinner please. Make her amazing darling. I see future generations from her, and what an amazing future they will be" Gyps smiled as she obeyed.

Liam walked behind the First Mates seat, "You could do a hell of a lot worse, but finding better maybe hard." The First Mate glanced at his face questioning his response as Liam winked his approval. Gyps escorted the First Mate out.

Liam approached Gran from behind and patted her on the shoulder as he bent down to hug and kiss her on the neck. "Congratulation's darling, you deserve the best and I think you both have done well."

He stood up to shake the hand, congratulate and thank the chairman, when the old man stopped him, stepped back and began speaking again. "You boys were taken from me once over 47 years ago, but I fought back. Then they tried to take baby Eli away and I fought back again. I know you can't see me as your grandfather but I have always seen and loved you two boys as my grandsons and so did your mothers' parents. So do you think after all these years I could possibly warrant a hug?"

Liam opened up an gave him the biggest hug he could manage as tears welled both men's eyes. "Your mum would be so proud of you boys."

Then Gran intervened "and your father would be so pissed off. Now that's what I call real justice." She stood beside her husband, slid her arm into his, winked at Liam as she said, "who'd a thought, the Pirate and the witch, has a nice ring to it don't you think?"

As they started walking out together, the chairman exclaimed, "you're no witch."

She answered, "well you're no Pirate either but it doesn't mean we wouldn't have made good ones."

Liam sat back in his seat in the room by himself. He indicated to the barman to give him another drink as he sat there unravelling the day's epiphanies. The entire days drama unfolded his life like some diabolical soap opera finally fitting all the pieces together, the good, the bad and the very ugly.

With tears in his eyes, he raised his glass to his mother. "You were always a wonderful mother and I loved you. Thanks for not giving up on us mum, and grand-dad," he paused, "I've now got a grand-dad mum," he laughed. "He did good mum he took care of us. He kept his word. He kept Eli safe; he kept me safe, mum. He did a really good job. Cheer's mum."

"Talking to yourself" echoed a small female voice from behind the bar.

He walked over beside stool in front of the bar. "Hello Gyps," He smiled so happy to see her again. "Been awhile," she concurred as she kept cleaning up the area. He reached for her hand as it was wiping the bar, "Stop for a minute please Gyps." He stared at her lovingly.

"Don't look at me like that, please." she begged

"Too late Gyps." He frustratingly indicated to the barman, "he can finish that, you come here, I need to talk to you." She hesitantly obeyed.

"I've missed you." he whispered as she tried to disregard his comment, he placed his finger across her lips, "shush, let me say this please."

"I loved my wife and I gave her everything I could to make her life happy and I think I succeeded, and after she died, she left me a letter saying she was my soul mate but she gave me permission to find someone until we were together again. For a long time, I believed that. Then I mentioned it to Eli and he went off like a rocket. He called her a controlling bitch and a manipulating cow and he said she was a female version of our father only I couldn't see it. He said that's what they do, they make out they are doing it for you, but it is only for them."

Gyps sat quietly gob smacked at his revelations.

I realise I, like Eli needed her at that time to get me here otherwise I wouldn't have made it, but I'm here darling, I made it back to you. The minute I saw you again this afternoon, I knew." He saw the curious look on her face, "it's always been you Gyps. I was blinded by her possessiveness, it was all I knew from my father, but you literally saved me. You've always had my back, probably for centuries too, like mum. My father, my wife divided me, I bent over backwards to make them happy and that made me feel worthwhile, but with you I'm already worthwhile, I'm complete with you."

"You marry many times but you only love once,"

"That's not correct," responded Gyps quietly.

Sitting upright she commenced, "It's a Romanic expression century's old. It's, 'you marry many times, but you can only love one; YOU."

She confidently continued, "We are actually incapable of loving anyone else. However, when you love you; truly love you, you wear that garment of love and then every thought, word and action is derived from that love and oozes out of you. You automatically synchronised with the same world of love surrounding you, but you've done nothing." She scanned his face, "and when you look into the eyes of someone who has that love, you can't take your eyes of them. They are all you see. It's has that unbelievable connection" Liam felt his heart leap out of his chest.

"I like mine better." He countered her with a huge smile, "I love you Gyps, you are my soul mate, you always were, there's no one else for me, there never will be. I knew that the minute I saw you again this afternoon and that toast the chairman," he paused realising his vocabulary mistake, "my grandfather made means you and me too." He re-positioned himself to be directly in front of her, "Gyps I have wasted hundreds of lives by bowing down to others and being their puppets, now it's time for us.

Please, my darling my beautiful Gypsy, marry me." He passionately kissed both of her locked hands.

"I did not see this coming," she responded.

"Not the answer I was expecting." He retorted.

"Oh no," she grinned as she coyly lowered her head. She had no words.

"Liam tried another angle, "When I'd fall in love in the past it was fast and explosive as if I needed it to make it past the next obstacle and they'd suck the life out of me until I petered out, but you had my back through it all Gyps and I never saw it till this afternoon. Think about it please, have dinner with me, join us all for dinner tonight?"

She declined saying "it's for your family."

"You know more about my family than I do," he contradicted.

"Dinner tonight with me please?"

She nodded, "now let me get back to work." And she scooted him out of the room. Gyps returned to the bar to an attendant with a huge smile. "You shouldn't eavesdrop."

Oh no mum, you can't stop hearing, but what happens in this menagerie stays in this menagerie. Mum if I may be pert, what he said to the other lady, 'you could do a lot worse, but you'll find it hard to do better He seems nice mum, and he seems sincere, after all these years you deserve this." He wiped the last glass and said "finished, now mum, you go look like a superstar, you deserve it." He then scooted her out of the bar and closed it down.

Thinking the worlds gone crazy, Gyps passed through the dining room requesting another setting for the table then retreated to her unit to prepare for the evening's entertainment and meal. She had a garment for such an occasion, she'd never worn it, never had the courage nor a reason, it always seemed inappropriate till now, like everything else; it too had to wait for the right time.

At the head of the table sat the patriarch and the matriarch, as the next generation entered one by one. Liam, followed by Eli both looking very debonaire. The gentlemen all rose from their seats as First Mate gracefully waltzed into the room and was seated by Eli. The expression on his face spoke volumes, he kissed her gently and complimented her attire, but words could not express what he was feeling.

Liam's world started spinning in slow motion and melted away as he beheld the vision of Gyps entering. She took his breath away. He was mesmerized by every flowing movement. Eli and the others saw his reaction to which Gran mumbled, "bout time."

Eli questioningly looked at Gran and she responded quietly, "that's been going on for nearly twenty years only they both just had walls of baggage to get through."

"But he was married?" he whispered.

"A little goss dear, if Gyps wasn't there keeping that woman in line, there wouldn't have been a marriage."

"The letter; she left a letter for Liam saying she was his soulmate his forever after. That was all Gyps," he continued whispering.

"The little tyrant," exasperated Gran, "neither of them would have realise Gyp's DNA was telling her she was his soul mate. Funny how things finally work out. As it should be."

She paused awhile "I always say I want to be there when it ends, but ending are only new beginnings, and you can't be round for all of them I guess." They both laughed

As Liam took Gyp's hand to guide her to her seat, she responded to his afternoon request, "yes." Liam gently took her face into his hands and without thinking softly kissed her lips

"Sorry Gran, Eli, I didn't think anyone would mind, if I invited Gyps to be my guest for dinner tonight." apologized Liam.

Eli stepped up and gave him a hug and Gran smiled with approval. "I've known about it for years." she smirked. Liam again was surprised at her comment. As she held her husband's hand. "From experience my dear, you don't get to be rewarded with a love like ours until you have eliminated all the debris that's preventing it. If I had mentioned it in any way, you would have torn it to shreds. No, it has to come to you, then not only do you understand it,you get to see how beautiful it is and why you deserve it. I presume by that timid 'yes' my dear that congratulations are in order?"

"Yes ma'am," came the coy response as Liam kissed her hand proudly.

She turned to Eli, "Now don't you go putting any pressures on…"

"Too late Gran," was Eli's rebuttal "I already asked her this afternoon."

"And," she questioned the First Mate hoping for a good response.

"I said yes ma'am."

As Gran threw up her arm and punched the air she grunted "yes, now where's that waiter? Looking at her husband, "this calls for a real celebration darling."

As the barman arrived, she sat back in an authoritive manner, "bring me the very best we have."

Her husband kissed her hand, "I love you girl." The boys looked at them in amazement for to see adults older than themselves expressing any feeling of love to one another was an unprecedented experience.

As the celebratory dinner commenced, they all began to unwind and vent the day's proceedings but more than anything else they all started sharing the warmth of what it was like to be a united family again. They shared sophisticated food and wine, lots of love and laughter.

Eli stood to give a toast, feeling overwhelmed by the sensation of his freedom, his future life and a little too much scotch. He began waving his hands around the table as he addressed them, "What we have here is an exceptional family, weird, but exceptional. "But this is my family now. I've never had one like this before and I never want to lose it." They all nodded in agreement. "I don't know how we got here but I'm glad we did."

"You Eli," echoed the quiet gypsy beside Liam. She suddenly gained a full audience, "You're the youngest, we are all following you. You are our future; we are your feedback."

"The murderer, you were all following a murderer." He despondently replied.

"No," she hesitantly replied, "same as this existence, you reacted to a murderer. I'd say you've experienced various prisons as well so the prison concept is important also, so you've reacted to many murders, and we've all followed until it was finished. This time it was finished. Now with the original obstacle relinquished, you were no longer imprisoned by it."

If you're going to teach freedom you have to know how you acquired it, understand it, be it. I think you will be brilliant on this path for no one knows it as well as you do but when and how did you receive it? What saved you?"

Eli indicated his mother but Gyps negated his answer informing him she was the aftermath of his awakening. "When you think of murder, hatred, imprisonment you think of your father. Who do you think of when I say love, saviour, enlightenment.?"

Eli looked at his brother Liam with love, pride and gratefulness.

"You came back for me man. You went into my hell and you saved me." Eli thought for a while as he recalled the events of that first week after his visit. "In one week, you took me from cold hearted nothingness to becoming excited to see you again."

Eli recognised that Gyps and Gran were going to tell him different, "yeah I know I'm the one who altered my genes, my cells, yeah I know that." He paused a moment. "Damn it's almost as if I can see it now. Every day, with every thought of Liam, I was shattering all the old, what, binary codes, and replacing them with new ones of him."

"Liam has always been this amazing love; I saw that with his wife. He followed you because he loved you. He was the only one who could reactivate that binary in you because of the bond between you two and the rest of us followed suit."

Liam interjected, "And that's why you have my back. You knew I was following him."

She grinned back to him, "Told you not to worry."

"So, I put my trust in the hands of a gypsy?" suspected Liam.

"Who else knows how to get you out of hell."

The Chairman remained in his seat as he spoke up and presented himself as patriarch of his new family. "A lot of those prisoners have walked the exact same path as you, son and I'm all for you going back and helping them, but to teach this will have you thrown out on your ear. However, knowing all this, bullshit as you call it, and how you cornered your personal freedom market and changed your life will give you an upper hand. With your brilliance and ingenuity, I see nothing but success for you both."

The Chairman asked then all raised their glasses, "Here's to starting again, again" He grinned as they shared his toast

Gran interceded, "Your grandfather and I make a toast every night to the safety and love of this family. I'm not going to ask you to do it but I would love you to join us. I don't want to lose any of you again either, so every night at sunset, where ever we are, we raise our glasses, our coffee's, our drinks, and toast to all of us being together forever." She raised her glass, "Only the best, for all of us, forever."

In agreement they all raised and clinked their glasses as they repeated.

"ONLY THE BEST, FOREVER."

Within days they parted and they all ventured far and wide. Gran and the Pirate travelled to Europe and settled in Greece. And every night at sundown on a lounge outside the front of their villa overlooking the most beautiful of clear blue waters they watch the sunset and declare their toast. They then snuggle up as aged lovers do and fall asleep in the warmth of each other's arms. Then as the night air gets cooler, they take each other off to bed.

Eli put together a platform where he, as part of The University Apprenticeship Program does motivational speaking and training for rehabilitation prisoners. His greatest supporter is the chairperson and she promotes his work through many of the co-joining rehabilitation centres for all ages.

He, his First Mate and baby daughter sail the seas and compete at every opportunity. Every sunset at the helm of their craft without fail where ever they are, they ardently declare a toast to the unison and love of their entire family, and future generations forever.

Liam joined Gyp's family of a son, daughter in law and a beautiful grand-daughter. He and Gyps own the resort and with her children they all now manage the very successful tourist facility which sponsors several national and international regattas. Come sunset every night, with his brand- new family, they all find a comfortable place together where they raise their glasses to the extended family and future successes for all that they too wish to share, and experience.

So, here's a toast to you and all your future lives. Raise your imaginary glasses

May you live with the people you love.

May you live the futures you desire,

May you experience true freedom to its fullest,

forever;

To all of us

ONLY THE BEST, FOREVER

EPILOGUE

THIS IS HOW IT WAS;

THIS IS HOW IT IS;

THIS IS HOW IT CAN BE.

Through Karma, all old philosophies and scripture we have to keep breaking the heart to awaken the heart. However, there is another way. But before you can experience the better way, you have to acknowledge you are a victim of your own creations, all of them all around you.

The laws of the universe were discovered after we created them.

Your surrounding world is the way it is, because you created it that way by reacting to your creation.

You change your world from what it is, to what you exist in by your reactions to your environment.

If you read the feedback of your world, you will discover the emotional tool you used to create it the way you see it.

If you allow the world to be as it is, finished, it informs you of your past constructive criticism.

Every moment we experience, a thought, word or action, which creates your own personal script for our own personal journey. We then syncopate all binary codes to those manifestations and attract to us opposite and like minds ready to repel. Then we react to our surroundings creating a new script for us to follow for our continued ongoing path made up of the same emotional reactions; that's life.

Karma is a long path of ups and downs on a wave of emotional dysfunction. The higher the wave the more intense the dysfunction. The ongoing physical alterations are not as immediate as originally determined centuries ago. The teachings were, we would create a disturbance and when we died, we would immediately transform into that disturbance thus return in your next life as that disturbance.

 However, feedback of our aging development today, has informed us that all continued existences are a gradual process. All continued transformations occur at the same pace throughout the entire universe. Our visual impression is small things alter faster, larger thins much slower. However, when you also add to the equation that every living thing is nothing but miniscule atoms, then you can comprehend that the transformation takes place at the same pace however the volume of the structure determines the time of the complete transfiguration.

One reactionary thought to any of our surroundings immediately alters all our binary codes as updates to adapt. Then your DNA binaries alter, followed by the binaries in every chromosome, then we physically alter to become that reaction. A temper tantrum to our hair starting to dry out and go grey. This can take 0.1seconds to twenty years. Our skin starts tearing down and becomes frail and starts maintaining wrinkles, our memory is not as good as it once was, our teeth need work. Our diet alters to compensate for the new binary alterations. Gravity starts to kick in and have a very strong hold on our physical appearance. We physically start altering immediately but slowly and all of it takes up to ninety years, more or less.

It's a long process. However new information now determines that the speed of that process does not alter even after death. This was one of the misgivings. The matrix of the universe alters at the same pace all year round so what that determined was even in death you as a cell do not accelerate but continue altering and developing at the same pace only as an invisible cell. As every individual live cell upgrades so do all the invisible cells as well. When we return, we are a brand-new manifestation of that cellular upgrade.

All predetermined paths are set in motion from one original judgement through a thought, word or action. It will then provide you with your emotional personality. Your personality will provoke all the necessary situations for you to react to in certain ways so you can achieve the final goals of your original accusations, through more of the same thoughts, words and actions.

This ongoing merry-go-round will take centuries. Then when all the dramas that you originally envisaged have been completed, and you are no longer victim to that past life emotional accusation, your slate is clean.

If you respond correctly and realise your entire life's fiasco is feedback only of what you have already created through past lifetimes, and they don't really have a hold on you for they are finished, you may realise now that you have a second chance at life. Every emotional performance by others exposed in front of you is a past life reaction you created. You simply have a choice as to whether you wish to be exploited by that old creation or walk a new path of freedom.

Nothing is here to harm you, nothing is here to hurt you, you do it all to yourself, for yourself, by yourself. You can only love yourself, no one else can feel it, but if you know how to truly love yourself, then you will know how to love another.

This new perception of life then alters the laws of the universe. Like attracts like and opposites repel. Now you attract like to you through similar binaries as feedback. You all experience the same happiness so all the people places and events around you are happy in the same manner. You treat them the way you want to be treated. You love them the way you want to be loved.

All our emotions are imprisoning judgements. Forgiveness for example is a judgement. You are assuming the world around you exterior to you. It is a threat to you so you react like the dog barking at itself in the mirror. You forgive because you believe someone needs your forgiveness, they have harmed you. But they are only informing you that you are the one harming yourself. They are informing you of the emotional garment you are wearing. Forgiveness like all emotions is a fraudulent fiasco of imprisonment.

<u>ALLOWANCE IS EQUALITY. ALLOWANCE IS FREEDOM.</u>

If you are seeking justice, you will never find it. It doesn't exist, but then neither does injustice. In a hundred years' time those words will be emojis. What will still exist however is your inner emotional turmoil of some thought of some emotional injustice. You again become victim to some emotion within you which will imprison you.

The emotional source of injustice is within you no one else and as a result, your entire binary world will reveal infinite amounts of varieties of the synopsis of injustice everywhere around you, for you to experience, for this is all you know and you will keep experiencing it until you allow that world of injustice to exist as it is, without you. That's equality, that's freedom.

Now you start living with the attitude of who you truly want to be. Your blasts from you past will expose you to the episodes that not only still determined your old personality but determine the path that particular personality would have taken.

Thoughts words and actions scenarios, people, experiences are all repeated at the same time, the same age, with the same impact only in opposite and equal value to you over and over again until you realise who is controlling who and alter it.

You meet people at the same time; you experience specific scenarios at the same time; you use the same words or the same words will be used, but the ongoing path of injustice will continue with or without you. It is simply a binary mathematical equation that exists. It will attract to it any cell with the similar binary equation from human to horse.

Regardless of our vanity, pride, ego, we are simply a piece of a much larger puzzle. We travel specific emotional paths designed by our binary history. Regardless of the world around you, the country around you, the town around you, the people around you, the house around you this is your binary code in physical format. The binaries of each emotion are syncopating our DNA every day of our lives through our thoughts, words and actions to maintain some ultimate journey.

The past can be determined through algorithms, science and history. Our surroundings reveal our present path then our immediate futures because we do not alter them. They are an ongoing continuum only upgrading to a different arena.

Through some emotional feeling we experience an injustice, inequality, lust, greed, jealousy; this attitude then determines your immediate path and your long-term journey; we unintentionally follow it. It then displays itself through the wars, impoverishment, illness, poverty, wealth, of your world situation explaining to you that you have been here before at the same time, same age and this is what you, through your thoughts, words and, actions created, now you can maintain your creation or let it ride to completion without you.

New research now determines what happens when you decide not to participate in the same malicious ongoing synopsis. When you decide not to be imprisoned by these emotional personifications and choose freedom instead.

You are using the same tools, your emotions. You still alter your binaries but the attitude this time is one of freedom; but freedom doesn't exist either. It is an emotional awareness of a word called freedom that exists. Is it enough to alter future paths for future generations because you are not imprisoned?

Through all my studies I've discovered that altering my perception of me personally from the inside to one of allowance, equality and freedom, my entire environment altered and displayed before me exactly the same more positive outlooks. No longer opposite and repelling. It also displayed new a new town, new people in my life and I in theirs with similar attitudes. They are a more energetic people, more creative people, happier people; and they all have an attitude like mine. This my new feedback of a future possibility I'm willing to accept.

Many inscriptions say you cannot change the world you can only change your world.

But with validation I can honestly say, if you change your world the world will change around you and it does change around you.

IMPRISONMENT IS FROM A REACTION.

VICTIMISATION IS FROM A REACTION.

AND IT DOESN'T MATTER WHERE YOU EXIST.

RECOGNISING THEM TAKES AWARENESS.

FREEDOM IS YOUR OTHER OPTION.